Australion Aborigines

Australion Aborigines

Dinkar G. Wagle

KALPAZ

Published by

Kalpaz Publications
C-30, Satyawati Nagar,
Delhi – 110052
Ph.: 011-47034999, 9811692060
www.kalpazpublications.com
E-mail: kalpaz@hotmail.com

Distribution Network
gyanbooks.com
India, USA, Canada, UK, Australia, France

ISBN: 978-93-5722-755-1 (PB)

First Published, 2024

Printed at: Gyan Press, Delhi.

Australion Aborigines
Author: Dinkar G. Wagle

CONTENTS

PREFACE

The original natives of Australia descended from groups that existed that country for the 400 -500 years ago. At the time of initial European settlement over 250 years ago, over 250 languages were spoken by the Aborigines. It is estimated today 120 languages still exist and remain in use.

About 50,000 years ago, a volcanic eruption from Indonesia spread around the world including the southeastern part of India which made habitation very difficult with extensive famine . A lot of people escaped in boats and went to Australia . This was a very tortuous ride where lots of people died. The survivors managed to land in Northern part of Australia . Their Indian heritage was detected by DNA examination in the past 20 years.

The Aborigines lived as forages and hunter –gatherers and the society was generally mobile and lived the lives of Semi-Nomadic people. This book is a compilation of the history of Aborigines and brings the readers an up-dated version of these original natives of Australia. I am one of the earlier Indians who discovered the Australian native sons and daughters who now number over a million people.

This writer believes the Aborigines use the word "Formative Epoch" known as "DREAMTIME" which stretches back hundreds of years ago and shown vividly in their paintings on rock walls or on regular walls which has resemblance to the old Indian art. The author strongly suggests an Indian expert on Arts and Drawings should visit these sites in Australia and study them carefully to ascertain their Indian origin.

PART - 1

PRIMITIVE RELIGION

As a student in England, I heard Bertrand Russell's speech on Religion and its history and since my own knowledge was primitive, I did not understand the speech too well but it stuck a chord which remained for the past many years until recently. In the past few weeks, I began my series on Aborigines in Australia and their religion took me back by 50,000 years. This was simply a revelation and Russell's speech came to my attention. Since I had difficult time to understand it many years ago, I read the speech as a beginner's step, followed by further research on religion for clarification. These next few articles are the result of my observations on PRIMAL Religion. For various reasons, the Primal Religion has been relegated as a minor position compared to other world known religions. I have many difficulties to understand this position and also great difficulty understanding the word PRIMAL which means PRIMITIVE. I am trying to rectify that position and hopefully convince you the Primal Religion is not only a great religion but should be counted along with other religions of this world. There is nothing PRIMITIVE about it.

I CONSIDER PRIMAL RELIGION IS AS ADVANCED AS OTHER RELIGIONS AND DESERVES THE SAME CONSIDERATION AS OTHERS. THIS IS THE MAIN PURPOSE FOR THIS ARTICLE. WHY ARE

OTHER RELIGIONS CONSIDERED "HOLY" BUT NOT THE PRIMAL RELIGIONS. WE PURPOSELY FAILED TO UNDERSTAND THE HOLY RELIGION OF THE TRIBAL PEOPLE, SIMPLE AS THAT.

PHILOSOPHY OF RELIGION

The philosophy of religion enjoys the World Status. Everybody agrees that Primitive or Primal religion has yet to acquire that status. I am trying to incorporate the Primal religion experience within the categories employed in the modern philosophy of various religions irrespective of whether such categories or notions are found within the Primal Religion themselves.(Politics and racial prejudice does not help my case)

Brief Discussion- Primal Religion

Several terms have been employed to describe: (a) Primitive (b) Tribal (c) Small section (d) Folk e) Native (f) Oral (g) Shamanistic (h) Archaic. All these terms are used interchangeably throughout in the last hundreds of years and everybody seems to categorize the Primal **Religion as a so-called religion not worth knowing and belongs to illiterate savages and ancient tribal people. In my opinion, those people who think that way do not know their own religion and are totally ignorant people to say the least. The so-called scholars all these years brought us to this silly stage because of their total incompetence and ignorance.**

Historically, the militarily strong and rich countries purposely named their own country's religion and other neighbors religions as of High Quality and those from Africa and Asia as Lower Religions. **HOW DID THESE IDIOTS KNOW SO MUCH ABOUT RELIGIONS. THEY DID NOT. BUT ASSUMED THEY DID. But their** classification has stood hundreds of years because OF the OPNION OF SO-CALLED SCHOLARS. The **"so-called educated**

people" never questioned the WISDOM of these experts. THE SAME THING HAS HAPPENED IN MANY OTHER RELIGIONS I KNOW FAIRLY WELL. (Incidentally, my knowledge of religions is still primitive) A VERY SIMILAR DUPLICITY HAS TAKEN PLACE UNDER THE PRETENSE OF KNOWLEDGE. IT IS VERY UNFORTUNATE THAT UNDER THE NAME OF RELIGION, ALL KINDS OF SILLY ACTS ARE BEING FOLLOWED AND NOBODY SEEMS TO QUESTION THEM AT ALL. I SEE THIS HAPPENING IN DIFFERENT RELIGIONS WITH IMPUNITY.

One of my main reasons in these series is to **elucidate the Primal Vision of God and in the sense of the various kinds of comparison instituted between them. It is obviousthatTHE NotionOf God is not exclusive to any one religion or civilizationbut is presentwith variations in all of them**. The major question is why Primal Religions are run down as if it does not belong to any civilized people and is good for the so-called **Uncivilized Tribal People**. Who gave the monopoly to any religion to be the only religion for civilized people. It is very unfortunate that people all over the World brought us today to this day which hardly makes sense. The only people who tried to bring some sense like **Bertrand Russell were called Atheists so people would not believe them. All major religions like Hinduism, Islam, Christianity and other religions try to make themselves look prominent. Historically, this idea of blowing** your religion beyond limits has been practiced for thousands of years and brought this world to untold miseries. IT IS MY CONTENTION THAT WE, THE PEOPLE OVER THE LAST MANY CENTURIES BROUGHT US TO THIS MISERABLE SITUATION, CALLING SOME RELIGIONS PRIMITIVE AND OTHERS HIGH AND MIGHTY.

THE NATION OF GOD BELONGS TO ALL THE HUMANITY AND THERE IS NO SUPERIORTY OF ONE

RELIGION OVER THE REST. AS A MATTER OF FACT, **I BELIEVE FIRMLY THE PRIMAL RELIGION IS THE BEST RELIGION OF ALL AND ALL OF US SHOULDADOPT IT AS OUR OWN. This is my CONVICTION AND AM TRYING OTHERS WILL NOT ONLY UNDERSTAND BUT CONVINCE THEIR FRIENDS.**

HISTORY OF RELIGION: There are a few Primal religions past or present I am aware of. This so-called religion started in Africa close to a million years ago. (This is scholarly Guess by well -known historians). I am not going to any details of Homo-Sapiens beginning of gathering to form tribes for survival. I begin after the modern man as we know grew up in the middle of Africa. Our ancestors were primitive, agricultural people who were closely linked with **NATURE** and its many variations such cyclones, storms, floods, diseases and famines. **BUT THEY RESPECTED NATURE.** There were many such groups in Africa and all of them had common elements:

(1) All had similar outlook towards Nature. There was no distinction between the Secular and Non-Secular.

(2) Everything was SACRED.

(3) They passed on their **TRADITIONS ORALLY from one generation to next. There are no written texts on this religion because the writing was not invented.**

(4) They expressed their **relationships with their God through Myths and Mythologies by oral transmission. Incidentally, this extra-ordinary** transmission of myths continued in Ancient India 12,000 years ago and when writing was discovered in about 5000 years ago, the writing as a mode of communication literally exploded by writing the Vedas which even today are not easy to understand. **These ancient people were very clever and**

tried to bring People closer to REALITY (NATURE). **Unfortunately, the knowledge of writing did not reach Africa** and consequently, people in other countries did not know of African advancement and this remained so for many hundreds of years. **The Color prejudice, the Slavery, the Western Colonialism all contributed to the MISUNDERSTANDING of the AFRICAN BACKWARDNESSAND HAS REMAINEDSO EVEN TODAY.** There is no exaggeration in saying that even today African or for that matter Asian greatness in many subjects hardly gets due attention. **BUT THE PRICE AFRICANS HAVE PAID IS ENORMOUS. THE ACHIEVEMEMNTS OF THE WHITE RACE IS EXAGGERATED FOLLOWED BY A VARIETY OF PUBLICATIONS TO MAKE SURE THE CLAIMS ARE UNDERSTOOD BUT NOT A WORD OF PRAISE OCCURS WITH AFRICANS AND OR ASIANS IN THE PAST MANY YEARS.**

Orality is one of the trademarks of Primal Religion. Their stories by themselves make it easy to understand the Spiritual and Moral lessons that are intended by them. Rather than explain what God is in literal terms, stories are woven with the Nature and animals to show what God is like. **Orality preserves the intent of the lessons. The written word is often taken literally and the essence of its meaning is lost in the lines.**

In this tribal world, the Tribe is central to the individual human beings. It is everything in the ECOSYTEM of the GROUP. IT IS ALL OF NATURE, HUMANS, ANIMALS AND OTHER OBJECTS, ANIMATE AND INANIMATE.

SPIRITS : These peoples placed a great emphasis **on SPIRITS in Everything. Everybody has his or her place in the TRIBE. Everybody is taught to honor everything within the TRIBE and TRIBAL ENTITY.**

Of all the gifts to mankind by God, then there is none greater than the presence of the Holy Spirit. This spirit has many functions, roles and activities. In each religion, Spirits **play a major role.**

ORIGIN OF HISTORY

The earliest evidence of religious ideas dates back to more than 1 million years ago. Archaeologists refer to apparent intentional burial of Home Sapiens as early as half a million years ago and existence of religious ideas.

Through the bulk of human evolution, humans lived in small nomadic bands practicing a hunter-gatherer life-style. The emergence of complex and organized religion can be traced to the period when the human absorbed their nomadic life style to begin farming during the Neolithic period (Approximately, 400,000 years ago). The transitions from foraging bands to states resulted in more specialized form of religion.

Traditional African religions is based on **ORAL TRADITION** which means the basic values and way of life are passed on from elders to younger generation. These **traditions are not Principles of RELIGION but a CULTURAL IDENTITY THAT IS PASSED ON THROUGH STORIES, MYTHS AND MYTHOLOGIES. (Incidentally, this basic idea was** copied by EVERY NATION since then). Even today, we pass on these stories to our younger generation. I need to stress that SYMBOLS, MYTHS and MYTHOLOGIES played a very vital part in the transmission and spread of religion. I personally believe mythology played a much more vital role than understood.

WHAT DOTHE FOLLOWERS OF RELIGION BELIEVE

The community is the most important **part of SOMEONE'S LIFE**. This community is made up of people who remember and share the same traditions and the individual only exists within a community and separation from that community is sometimes worse than death. As I understand, this tradition was strictly followed by all he TRIBES IN AFRICA. Apparently, the tradition began in Central Africa and then spread EASE and WEST. Remember now, the world was still a small place and there was hardly any travel. ALL THESE PEOPLES IN AFRICA BELIEVED IMPLICITLY IN GUIDANCE OF THEIR ANCESTORAL SPIRITS. (I have not figured out why they placed so much emphasis on Ancestors and history. It is possible their own existence is due to their ancestors.)

They asked their ancestors to communicate with the Supreme on their behalf. The Supreme being is called upon in times of great hardships like famine, deaths, epidemics that threaten their entire community.

THE SUPREME BEING IS THE CONNECTION BETWEEN THE PEOPLE AND THEIR ENVIRONMENT. WE SHOULD OBSERVE THIS OUR GOD AND SUPREME BEING.

ANCESTRAL WORSHIP

This worship and belief is an extension of a belief in and respect for elders. Followers of traditional African religion believe that Ancestors maintain a Spiritual Connection with their living relatives. As I wrote earlier, the Primal Religion is usually pre-scientific and subjects like Ancestral worship is considered seriously without any arguments or discussions.

As I understand other religions, I do know similar devotions exist in every religion and nobody seems to mind it but when the Primal Religions are considered, every facet of that religion is considered seriously AND PURPOSELY MISREPRESENTED. WHY SO?

This will be continued in my next article.

References

1. E.E. Evans –Pritchard : Witchcraft, Oracle and Magic — Oxford University Press 1937.
2. M. Eliade : The sacred and the profane - Amazon Publishers - 2001.

PART - 2

PRIMITIVE RELIGION

In Part 1, we covered some of the details of the Aboriginal Primal Religion. To understand the religious and spiritual practices of these people, we need to establish how their mind-set differs from that of industrial and technological society like our own. The primal consciousness has not been attended by the condition and dichotomies of modern society. As a result, the primal religion is not fragmented but **remains WHOLE. All of the life is a symbolic paradigm of the SACRED**. These people make no distinction between craft, art, work and religion. As some experts vouch "You can start anywhere, with painting, dancing, poetry, songs or other artifacts".

TRADITIONAL RELIGION

The Aboriginal religion in Australia shares many similarities with that of Africa, yet they are distinctively different as the variety of Aboriginal languages. In the traditional Cosmology is AWARENESS among some tribes of a Deity such as THE ALL FATHER OR MOTHER. A lesser but more significant is the widely known THE RAINBOW SERPENT. This idea of a serpent and a variety of formative Spirits Being were as responsible for the formation of the present World Order.

There are many questions when I approach the question of religion in Africa with the assumption of UNITY or Multiplicity. And I am faced with many religious differences manifestations of a Coherent African Religion? I do not believe a single African Religion exists through the entire Continent. There is, however, a growing consensus that **UNITY is a better way of Conceptualizing about religion in Africa. I believe this to be true simply because Africa was divided widely and differences were successfully avoided to create UNITY.**

As I understand, starting from Ancient Times, African religions is the set of World Views, beliefs, symbols, traditions and various practices. It is very likely that the African Religion evolved without **"FOUNDERS" or "REFORMS"**, growing and spreading spontaneously in different parts of the Continent. It is also possible and experience as well as Reflection of the peoples in their TOTAL life situation setting. **I DID NOT COME ACROSS ANY BOOK ON AFRICANRELIGION TO GUIDE ME BUT THEIR RELIGION IS WRAPPED UP IN ORAL TRADITION AND CULTURES.**

From very old times, their RELIGION took shape unperceptively. As the people multiplied, they shared knowledge and skills. I believe THIS WAS THE CREATIVE PROCESS THAT TOOK PLACE SPONTANEOUSLY, ACCORDING TO CHANGES THAT ADDED NEW IDEAS AND PRACTICES AS WELL AS ABANDONING THOSE THAT ARE NO LONGER APPLIED.

IN AFRICA, THE RELIGION IN THE BROADEST SENSE MERGED INTO TOTAL EXISTENCE OF THE DIVERSE PEOPLES. (These conclusion are mine only and I came to it after studying the beginning of THE VEDISM 4000 years ago –I will deal with this subject more later).

AFRICAN RELIGIONS

Since these religion were the first ones in the World, there are many versions of this story. I gather there are FIVE PARTS to their Religion.

1. **BELIEFS:** The way people think about the Universe and their attitude towards LIFE ITSELF.
2. **RELIGIOUS OBJECTS**

A traditional DEITY in many African tribes

3. **VALUES and MORALS:** This m deals with ideas that safeguard or uphold the life of people in their relationship with ONE ANOTHER and the WORLD around them.

5. UNIVERSE : THIS IS SEEN AS ETERNAL CIRCLES AND ARE SYMBOLS THE CONTINUITY OF THE UNIVERSE. (the pictures on the next page).

DIFFERENT PRIMALRELIGIONS

In all cases, there is Human Relationship with the NATURE.

- Animism is found in Oral Religions
- There is a belief that there is a life force in all THINGS.

- Animals may be seen as RELATIVES
- ORIGIN: The supernatural or from stories of the Earth arising of previous Earths or from earlier chaotic forms

GODS: is often a higher God and resides in Shrines or temples

There is a link between Natural and Supernatural and there is no perceived division between them.

I THINK, THEREFORE, I AM : BY RENE DESCARTES (1630)

Long before Rene Descartes described this phrase, the Africans thought and practiced this saying through their entire lives. They believed implicitly in their being here for some good cause and were asked to obey the laws of Nature. I think there is a real question to understand how their MINDSET differs from that of industrial societies. One thing is absolutely clear. OUR PRIMAL CONSCIOUSNESS HAS BEEN ALTERED BY THE CONDITIONS AND DICHOTOMY OF MODERN SOCIETY WHILE THEIRS DID NOT.

I believe these Primal Religions have the true characteristics to form a religion closer to Nature than our famous modern religion have.

The Oxford Dictionary defines Religion as "Human Recognition of Superhuman controlling power and especially of a personal God or Gods entitled to OBEDIANCE and WORSHIP. This definition brings out two important aspects : (1) How does one distinguish Religion from Magic. And (2) Do these Primal religions have a doctrine of SALVATION.

The answer to the first question is NO and the second one is YES.

THEISM

In all Primal religions, there is no IMAGE WORSHIP. Let me quote from S. Mtibi, a famous African author;

In the beginning, was God

Today is God

Tomorrow will be God

Who can make an image of God

He has no body?

This quote is from MirceaEliade's book (Primal religions of Aborigines and quotes Mtibi).

It is true to say that these tribes in Africa or in Australia and other parts of the World preserve a DIRECT and CONCRETE connection with the SKY and the WORLD of STARS and METEORS. ALL THESE MAKE THE UNIVERSE AND CREATED MAN. IN THEIR SHOIRT STAY ON EARTH, THEY REVEALED MYSTERIES AND INSTITUTED CIVIL AND MORAL LAWS. THEY ARE GOOD(THEY ARE CALLED OUR FATHER). THEY REWARD THE UPRIGHT AND DEFEND MORALITY.

BUT NOWHERE**DOES THE BELIEF ON GOD OR SUPREME BEING DOMINATE THE RELIGIOUS LIFE. THE CHARACTIRSTICS OF PRIMAL RELIGIONS IS NOT THE BELIEF IN HEAVENLY BEING BUT TOTEMISM.**

CONCLUSIONS

THE DYNMAIC RELAITY OF A RELIGION IN PRIMITIVE CULTURES IS OBVIOUS WHEN WE CONSIDER ITS DIFFERENTIAL UNIVERSATILITY OF EXISTENCE.

SYMBOLS AND FEW CHARACTISTICS OF TRIBES (AFRICA AND AUSTRALIA)

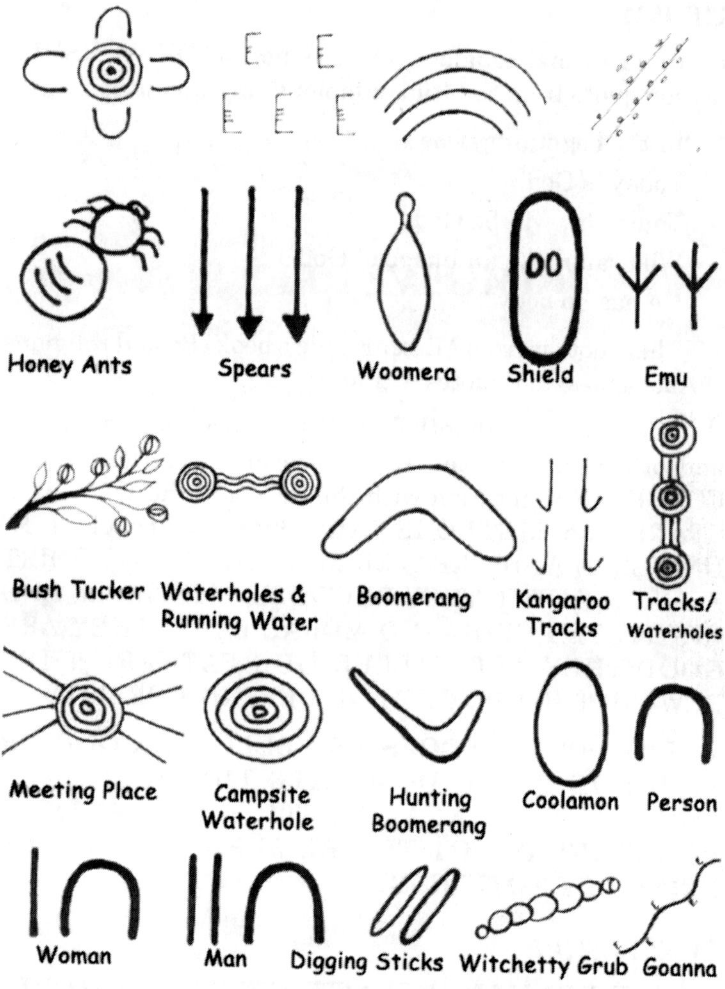

References

1. MerceaEliade: A history of religious ideas-Amazon Publishers-2001.
2. Hiatt, Lester: Arguments about Aborigines— Cambridge University press 1996.

PART - 3

PRIMITIVE RELIGION

ABORIGINES CULTURAL HERITAGE

KIDS AT SECONDARY SCHOOL

PHOTO OF NYADVANDAY SPIRIT CHILDREN

(Reference: Australian Government cultural heritage publication-2008)

As one of the oldest living peoples on Earth, the culture of Aborigine is rich, complex and enduring. The well-being of the people is connected to the land. Human kind's most ancient stone technology, the percussion methods of chipping away at the edge for cutting dates back 2 million years and now being practiced in Australia. Those flaked tools are used to shape wooden weapons such as a boomerang and other instruments. The manufacture and use of ground edge axes dates back at least 40,000 years in Papua New Guinea which was then attached to Australia.

ANCIENT INDIAN MIGRATION TO AUSTRALIA

I have borrowed the following information from "indigenous aboriginal and Torres strait islanders, 2013 – Government of Australia.

A new study of Indigenous Australian DNA suggests there was some form of migration from India to Australia as early as 50,000 years and late as 4000 years ago. Researchers had previously thought them isolated from the rest of the World for thousands of years.

A German study may change that assumption after it analyzed about 1 million genetic makers in Aborigines and compared the patterns variation to other populations such as British isles and other Europeans. Doctor Mark Stoneking of Max **Planck Institute for evolutionary Anthropology and a team of researchers found the first signs of Indian influence coincide with a time of significant developments to the way the Aborigines lived**.

Dr. Stoneking says there are two explanations for this link : It could have been by people actually moving from India to Australia or their genetic material could have moved in terms of contact between India and the neighboring populations who then had contacts with other neighbors and eventually had contacts with Australia. "The date that we get for when this gene flows from India occurs does coincide remarkably well with the first appearance of Microliths – the small stone technology – in the archaeological record for Australia" Dr. Stoneking stated. "It is possible all of these events are connected".

SUGGESTIVE TIMING

Professor Alan Cooper, from the University of Adelaide's Center of DNA says **the Indian influence may have played a significant role in the development of the Aborigine culture." The timing of all those things in the archaeological record about 5000 years, happens to match the timing of influx from India.**

Prof. Cooper also adds to another important development that happened around the time of this **Indian connection — a big expansion of one of the Aborigines language groups. "HOW DID IT REPLACE THE OTHER LANGUAGES" IS A BIG MYSTERY.** Dr. Stoneking states it has taken 5000 years to discover the Indian influence because the Aborigines have been very reluctant to talk of their ancestors and **ARE SUSPICIOUS OF EUROPEANS MEDDLING IN THEIR HOLY ANCESTRAL HISTORY". (I think this is an excellent** opportunity for the Indian Government to step in to start connecting with our past history.

MUNGO MAN (45,000 YEARS OLD)?

MORE INSIGHTS OF ABORIGINES ANCESTRAL HISTORY

In 1974, scientists digging a dry bed of Lake Mungo uncovered a skeleton of a Human preserves in the dry bed of sand and clay. Dating techniques revealed that this person died about 45,000 years ago.

The scientist and the press dubbed him as the **"MUNGO MAN"**. Why did he make such a splash? Not only because he was one of the oldest and complete skeleton of the earliest Australians but the discovery of the Mungo Man meant that the Australia was settled much earlier than many people thought.

This has been some archaeological and genetic evidence of a migration. But in a new study led by some anthropologists from India, geneticists believed that the migrants came from the East coast of India. This splendid work was carried out led by Mr. Satish Kumar of the Indian Anthropological society.

(Source: Aboriginal genetic study from Australian Geographic Society 2005)

CONCLUSIONS: In the past few years, more Aborigines are convinced and are participating in the research conducted by the Governments and Research institutes to trace the origin of these Aborigines. As I mentioned earlier, this is the right opportunity for the Government of India to take an active part to train our young scientists in RESEARCH such as anthropological, genetic etc.

References

1. Josephine Flood : Archaeology of the Dreamtime—J.B.Publishing Co. 2008.
2. Willerslev, Eske andNielsen, Ramusen: Science magazine Sept. 2011.

PART - 4

THE CULTURE AND CUSTOMS OF AGES PAST

PRIMAL (PRIMITIVE) RELIGION

A TYPICAL PICTURE OF PEOPLE FOLLOWING PRIMAL RELIGIOUS CEREMONY – WESTERN ABSURDITY AT ITS BEST.

When **the Western Press** wants to show other religious ceremonies apart from Christianity, I see nothing but pure mockery and extravagant absurdities. The so-called Primal or the Primitive religious picture shown above is a classic example of this total non-sense. **WHY DOES THE WESTERN CULTURE RUNS DOWN OTHER CULTURES AND SOCIETIES? One would expect these so-called European experts on History and Civilization would learn to RESPECT other religions and culture in its greatness and not just make fun of it. It shows a great disserice to the REST of THE WORLD and total ignorance on the part of some people. You can run them down AT YOUR OWN PERIL. IN THE LAST FEW YEARS, THE WHITE PREJUDICE HAD SUBSIDED A LOT BUT HAS ONCE AGAIN REVIVED ITS PACE WTH TRUMP' ELECTION. IT IS SO UNFORTUNATE THAT THESE IGNORANT PEOPLE ARE SIMPLY RUNNING DOWN THEIR OWN CIVILIZATION TO THE GROUND AND THEY ARE NOT EVEN AWARE OF IT. (Ref. 1)**

BASIS OF PRIMAL (PRIMITIVE) RELIGION (AUSTRALIA)

Many Primal people are Earth bound which means **the Divine is** everywhere and dwells in everything. This is at **the HEART of the RELIGION**. Trees, animals, water, rocks, mountains are thought of having Spirits or being DEITIES. In my limited knowledge, Primal Religions are generally based on an understanding for the world that is limited to a culture's Specific Geographical location. It also turns out that the other **well - known religions base their philopsophy on the PRIMAL RELIGION. IT IS MY OPINION, THAT MOST WESTERN WRITERS OFHISTORY AND RELIGION SEEM NOT TO BE AWARE OF THIS FACT AND THEY ARE SIMPLY NOT AWARE OF WHAT THEY DO NOT KNOW. There is a widespred absence of knowledgein the Western World of other cultures** and activities and a large tendency to criticise it simply because it came from non-white background. How do we educate these ignorant people in U.S. and Europe and bring everybody along the path of sound knowledge and understanding. The RICHNESS of a country has always played a decisivce role for the last thousands of years and today is no exception. Most of these countires are very poor and since they do not form the majorit to reckon with, they and their culture and religion are looked down without any solid reason except they are not wealthy. **An absolute shame! WEALTH OF A PERSON OR A NATION IS THE ONE AND THE ONLY REASON TO FIND MY ASSERTION ABOUT THE RICHNESS OF ANY CULTURE. (I mentioned this fact many times in my articles that Greece always borrowed ideas like DEMOCRACY, mythological stories, religion etc. from India and Iraq but Western historians never even mentioned these facts once. All these inventions were ascribed to Greece and to Rome. Glory to the TRUTH of these writers. All their Civilizations were based on the Indus Valley in India and The Mesopotamian in the Middle East.(Ref. 2 and 3).**

It is very unfortunate that my efforts to give due credit has not worked out well. Perhaps, some younger generation would hopefully ask for due reognition.

A BITTER EXPERIENCE

The education and means to bring the **iliterate Aborigines** along with very bright Australians is ons sad story of the last century.

This is of the Russian experiment conducted in 1950 or so. The Communists found that the entire Russian government, its science and other programs were run by very few elites and highly educated of the Communist society. They tried to correct the situation by picking kids of 2 years and older from **working classhomes** and put these kids with other kids in special dormitories to bring their education at the same level as the elites. These kids of ordinary citizens got the best education **but socially they did not belong to any society**. They did not like their parents nor top authorities. Ten years later, the Government realied its mistake and abandoned its entire program at a very high cost. **The lesson is you cannot impose "NEW CULTURE" at will. It is high time the Australian Government learns of this disastrous Russian experiment.**

KILLING WITHOUT MURDER : (My sincere thanks to Ms. Schimel of Lehigh University for the title and her essay on the subject). The title aplies to our situation: the **Aborigines History is written by the Victorious**, History tells us. This applies well in every respect with the unfortunate Aborigines. In this case, the entire history is written by the White settlers from the British islands, the **Victors.** From as Far back as 1814 and until 1980, Australian Government were forcibly removing Aboriginal children from their families with the intention of remolding them to become a part of the White Society. Regardless of good intentions whether they were or not benevolent, **the main aim was toEliminate Aborigines as a class**. Forthunately, the entire **experiment FAILEDMISERABLY. Simply put, Australia's asimilar policy in the 20th century as embodied by the Stolen Generation has contributed to biologicaland socio-cultural genocide.**

"We may go home, but we cannot relive our childhoods. We may reunite with our relatives but we cannot achieve 30-40 years without their love andcare." –(the Russian report and a similar report by the Aborigines). I am waiting for the Autralian report on this experiment.

WORKING VALUES

It is important to remember that the ideology, language and the value system of the stolen generation time period was very different 50 years ago than today. There were two important parts to these experiments:

ABSORPTION: Unlike the Soviets, the ultimate disappearnce of the Aborigines Race was to be realized in two ways: Biological absorption and Socio-Cultural Assimilation. The first was through attempted Control of their Birth and Death rates. European White Race policy has long been adopted officially by their governement.

ASSIMILATION: The idea is to eradicate the cultures of the Aborigines people throiugh a program of Assimilation into white culture to the end that no Australian would look, act, speak about Aborigines. **How can a government decide to eliminate the memories of their original people? What kind of JUSTICE is this. (Ref. 1)**

VICTORS CAN DO NO WRONG. Australia is considered as on of the most advanced countries in the world!

As of today, none of these policies have worked well.There is fear that another STOLEN GENERATION is growing as the children of the original stolen generation is running into trouble with the law.

IT IS MY SAD EXPERINCE THAT THESE WESTERN COUNTRIES INCLUDING AUSTRALIA ARE TRYING TO IMPOSE THEIR WILL IN THE MIDDLE EAST BUT FOR SOME REASONS DO NOT DO ANYTHING TO ERADICATE CLASS DISTINCTION IN THEIR OWN COUNTRIES.

THE COMPLEX STRUCTURE OF THE ABORIGINES GROUPS

As I went through various Civilizations dating back 10,000 years to the present, I came across many diffeent types of complex systems from Hierarchical, self-similar,or fractal like sturctures that have endured to maximize their internal efficiency. That was the matter of Survival and Prosperity. The Aborigines, as I understand, have 1189 social groups in 340 societies. They arw embedded within a complex eco-system that is well- organised at multiple scales by the exchanges of matter between organisms and its environment, (Schneider and Kay - 2007). These groups harvest resources to meet metabolic and material requuirements by ADJUSTING GROUP SIZES. **An astonishing achievement by these groups**. (Ref. 2)

DEGRADING ABORIGINES

Let me go back to the beginning of my article where Aborigines are shown in degraded form such as stupid dances, dresses and, manners that make look ridiculous. I have lived and travelled in the Western World for over 60 years and never saw any picture or a story that showed how stupid some of the European customs are. **But when it comes to anything non-white, all the fun begins and make them look ridiculous and in a way, degraded to show superiority of white race agianst every body else.**

Hollywood version of "How the West was won" relied totally on the presence of native tribes of Indians who were wiped out or reined in by the cleverness of the Whites. As a matter of fact, there was no single American Indian in all these films. The Indian parts were filled by **Darkskinned Italians or Spaniards who talked in a funny language to make people laugh and make theNatives look idiots**.This portrayal of dark skinned Natives has become the SYMBOL of WHITE SUPREMACY. ALL THESE MEDIA COMPANIES WHO MADE POTS OF MONEY AT THE EXPENSE OF RACIAL INJUSTICE.

Same thing happened in Australia.The Aborigines are being portrayed as Primitive, illiterate,volatile,devious or passive and sub-missive in films and TV shows. (general information). Such depictions have become comfortable frame of reference for most of us each time there is a question about these Natives. Just to remind our readers, English have made this color prejudice as their semi-official national policy in Asia, Africa and now in Australia.

MISREPRESENTATION

It hurts me to write this because there is no need to hurt these innocent people. There is too much image **of the Whiteness of Australia and** its government for the past hundred years. A general climate of "Political Correctness" has dovetailed with genuine efforts in the last few years—but very subtle vestiges of Native stereotypes still remain in this world and Australia is no exception.

HISTORICAL INACCURACIES

Films and TV shows have never let details get in the way of a good story. They are there to enteratain you and make money. Truth hardly matters. Nowhere is this truer than in depiction of Aboriginal Life where artistic license is liberally applied in portraying dress,customs and piritual beliefs and ceremonies. **THIS REDUCTION OF CULTURAL HERITAGE AND DIVERSITY AND AN UNNECESSARY YET SYSTEMATIC WAY OF PERPETUATING ERRONEOUS STEREOTYPES.**

WHY DOES ANY WESTERN GOVERNMENT PERSIST IN SHOWING THE SUPERIORITY OF ONE RACE AGAINST THE OTHER. IT IS SIMPLY IN THE INTEREST OF THE MONIED, HIGH POWER WHITE CULTURE.

The most erroneous flagrant omissionin Australia's TV shows is the Aboriginal Women. When she is included in the show, she is most often as a "Sexual Savage" with the implication she can be tamed and therefore, degraded.

Perhps, the most destructive to the image of the Aborigines people is the lack of character and personality and apparently shown on TV frequently. These people are always in suporting roles or regulated to the background and rarely speak as if they do not understand simple English.

I never went to Australia but am writing this after reading many, many columns on this subject. Please believe me, this story is sad, very sad. May be I feel spiritually and **Ancestral wise closer to these Aborigines, and hence, my few caustic remarks.**

References

1. Houston Smith: The World's religions - Harper San Fransisco 1991.
2. Carol Myss: Sacred controls – Harper publications 1995.
3. S. Mtibi : African Wikipedia – Africn tribes.

PART - 5

PRIMITIVE RELIGIONS

EVOLUTIONARY FORMS OF RELIGION- Section 1

PHOTO OF MOTHER GODDESS FLANKED BY TWO LIONESSES (10,000 YEARS AGO- TURKEY)

INTRODUCTION

The emergence of Religion and religious behavior during the Neolithic period (500,000 years to 150,000 years ago) brought about evidence of Spirituality or Cultic behavior prominently. I wanted to know the connection between the origin of Religion in Tribal Africa where it continued for hundreds of years and its sudden emergence in Australia 50,000 years ago. How was the TWO SIMILAR RELIGIONS appear in two separate parts of the World in almost identical forms separated by hundreds of years. My major focus was to find the connection between the two and the emergence of other religions after that. Is there a common element that binds these two Primitive religions and then can we find some commonality to other religions that followed. I do not have that answer. This mystery is yet to be solved.

THE ORIGIN OF MAN'S RELIGION

What is the origin of Man's religion? Why does every culture in this world worship some Divine being? Anthropologists and historians have studied this question and presently, there are some primary theories.

In the Subjective Theory, human have a psychological need for a transcendent being that provides **HOPE and meaning to their EXISTANCE.** Adherents believe that this religion makeup exists below our conscious awareness. Cultures have various views of Reality according to our experience. This disposition lies in our sub-conscious. In other words, our beliefs about a transcendent being are not the result of external realities but they came from our psyches. These feelings are expressed through our Symbols and religion.

In the East coast of India, there lives a tribal group called the Santal People about 12,000 years ago and were found to worship elements of Nature just like the Tribes in Africa half a million years ago and the Aborigines 50,000 years ago. Before their practices developed, they worshipped Thakur Jiu, their genuine God who created all things. Although they know Thakur Jiu was their true God, they stopped worshipping Him and instead worshipped the Nature. (The Santals are a part of Austro-Asiatic group. closer to Vietnamese people).

In Ethiopia, the people sacrificed to evil spirits out of fear. However, their god was Magano, the ONE OMNIPOTENT CREATOR.(Joe Kitigawa—the history of religion— Mc Millan publishers 1985). If there is a pattern in following any religious beliefs, it is not clear from these examples. But one concept is clear: People do want to worship some identity different from themselves.

According to Professor Dunbar, one of the World's best anthropologists, religion arose as mechanism to facilitate Social Cohesion (started with Primitive People of Africa and perhaps, of the Aborigines). This was done to ensure that these communities provided the Ecological benefits they were intended to provide. Justin L. Burette in "Why Would anyone believe in God" suggests that belief in God is NATURAL because it depends on our MENTAL TOOLS persevered by all Human Beings, super-powerful and Immortality highly attractive. (Burette: Oxford University Press 2007).

RELIGIONS IN THIS WORLD : As of 2014, there are an estimated 4200 different religions in the world today and are characterized as Primitive (Primal) religion followed by Hinduism, Christianity, Islam, Buddhism and Judaism as shown below.

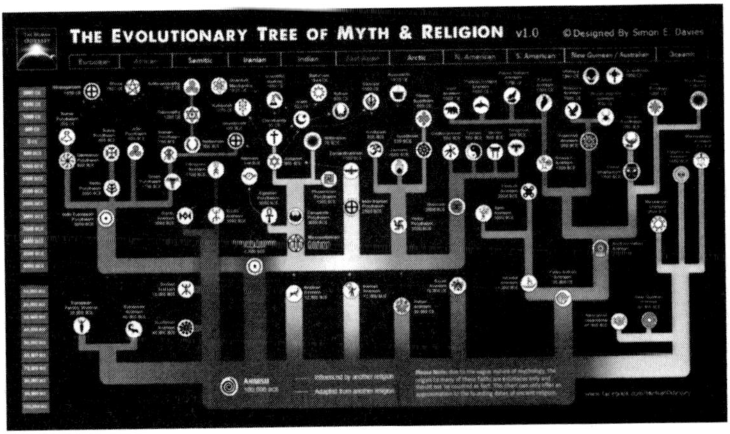

(Courtesy of THE WORLD PRESS, 2011)

We are dealing with the period of 500,000 years to 50,000 years ago and covers both the African as well as the Aborigine period. The main MYSTERY is the apparent similarity between the two, one in Africa and the other in Australia separated by half the World around and its slowdown (not the Demise) is very surprising. This anomaly brings out all kinds of questions. As the chart suggests, there is a great deal of similarity of the creation and existence of various religions. I will try to follow this lead to uncover the mystery of the existence for all these religions but for the present, my main focus is on the Primitive religions and how did it interact with other religions. Just to remind readers the African Primitive religion is not active while the aborigines' religion is still active and fully participated by followers.

PRIMITIVE (PRIMAL) RELIGION: As I stated earlier, Professor Dunbar of Cambridge University conducted a pioneering research work over a number of years and it literally overwhelmed me with my primitive knowledge.

Dunbar and other experts like Barbara King of Oxford University started with the Chimpanzees, bonobos and human background and established the basic facts that the Human Being has a much larger Brain size than others.

SOCIAL EVOLUTIONOF HUMANS

PERIOD YEARS AGO SOCIETY TYPE NUMBER OF INDIVIDUALS

100,OOO -10,000 BANDS 10 TO 100'S

10,000 - 5,000 TRIBES 100'S TO 1000'S

50000-, 3000 CHIEFDOMS 1000 TO 10,000'S

3,000 - 1,000 STATES 10,000 TO 100,000'S

2,000 -PRESENT EMPIRES 100,000 TO MILLIONS

SETTING THE STAGE FOR HUMAN RELIGION :

INCREASED BRAIN SIZE:

In this set of theories, the religious mind is one consequence of a BRAIN that is one of consequences of a Brain is large enough to formulate religious and philosophical ideas. During human evolution, **the Hominid Brain TRIPKED in SIZE, peaking half a** million **years ago. Much of the Brain's expansion took place in the NEOCORTEX. This part of the Brain is involved with human religiosity.** The Neocortex is also involved to self-consciousness, language and emotions. According to Dunbar's theory, the relative neocortex size of any correlates with the social complexity of particular species.

Professor Dunbar further argues that the expansion was the highest ever recorded. Professor Gould of Oxford University that Religion may have grown out of this expansion.

TOOL SIZE: Professor Wolpert of Cambridge University and an expert on Human psychology argues that the casual beliefs that emerged from played a major role in the evolution of belief. The manufacture of complex tools requires higher sophistication supplied by the brain.

DEVELOPMENT OF LANGUAGE: Religion also requires a system of Symbolic communications, such as language from one individual to another. Nicholas Wade (Before Dawn, discovering the lost history of our ancestors— Penguin Books 2001) "Like most behaviors that are found throughout the World, religion has been present in the ancestral human population before the dispersal from Africa 50,000 years ago. Although religious rituals have dance and music, they are also very verbal since the sacred TRUTHS have to be stated. If so, religion, at least in its modern form, cannot pre-date the emergence of language. It has been argued earlier that language attained its modern state shortly before the exodus from Africa. If religion had to wait the evolution of modern, articulate language, the it would have emerged shortly before 50,000 years ago".

Perhaps, we have that distinguishes individual religious beliefs from collective religious beliefs. While he former does not require the language, the latter does. This activity predates by far the emergence of langua

SINCE THIS ARTICLE IS GETTING TOO LONG, I WILL CONTINUE IN MY NEXT.

PART - 6

PRIMITIVE RELIGIONS

SUB-HEADING: EVOLUTIONARY FORMS OF RELIGION - SECTION 2

In my last article (part 5), Professor Dunbar's monumental work on Brain Size during the Neolithic period (200,000 years ago) which provided the main support to establish a Religion among the Primitive People of Africa. I introduced that as an example to the emergence of religion with the Aborigines of Australia 50,000 years ago. It was not a coincidencebut the environmental aspects in both these cases were very similar if not identical. Only the humans developed such a Brain Size and not Chimpanzees as they data suggest. As far as we know today, the thinking power of a certain size of brain is essential to form the rudiments of a religion.

I find this monumental discovery absolutely Amazing. Nobody to the best of my knowledge had defined the scholarly reasons for establishing a religion. Scholars talked about this subject but never did I see such massive and scientific data as produced by Dunbar and his team. This opens up an entirely new avenue for further research. All of us should insist on understanding the basics of that high importance. FOR THE FIRST TIME, I UNDESTAND

THE REASONS FOR THE PRIMITIVE AND SUBSEQUENT RELIGIONS. EACH RELIGION WAS AN AWSOME DISCOVERY, REGARDLESS OF ITS REASONS, GOOD OR BAD.

INCREASED BRAIN SIZE: Religious mind is one consequence of a Brain Size that is large enough to formulate religious and philosophical ideas (Proceedings of the Royal Society –Sept. 2011). During human evolution, the Hominid Brain is involved in processing higher order cognitive function that are connected with human religiosity. Since Dunbar's theory states that the relative Neocortex size of any species co-relates with the level of social complexity of the particular species. In Chimpanzees and bonobos, the neo-cortex occupies 50% of the brain while in Humans, it occupies 80-85% of the brain. This neo-cortex correlates with a number of social variables such as group size and mating behaviors. WE CAN FURTHER ARGUE THAT THE CRITICAL EVENT, THE EVOLUTION OF NEO-CORTEX TOOK PLACE AT THE SPECIALIZTION OF ARCHAIC HOMO-SAPIENS ABOUT 500,000 YERASG AGO. Most of the articles I have come across support this basic theory. As far as I know, there has been no exceptions or contrary opinions on this fundamental research. **BRILLIANT WORK.**

MORALITY AND GROUP LIVING

Prof. Barbara King (Dynamic Dance– Cambridge University press, 2004) view human morality as having grown out of Primate Sociality. Though morality awareness may be a unique human trait, many social animals have known to exhibit pre-moral sentiments which include retaining individual selfishness and building co-operative groups. For any social groups, the benefits of being a part of a group outweighs the benefit of individualism. All these animals including the Humans develop social order and hierarchy.

EVOLUTIONARY PSYCHOLOGY OF RELIGION

THERE IS GENERAL CONSENSUS AMONG SCIENTISTS THAT RELIGION IS AN OUTGROWTH OF BRAIN ARCHIECTURE THAT EVOLVED EARLY IN HUMAN HISTORY. However, there is some disagreements on the exact mechanism that drove the evolution of the Religious Mind. The two main schools of Thought hold the view that the religion evolved **due to natural selection and has selective advantage or that religion is an evolutionary by-product of other mental adaptations.** For this article, I am not going into details of this debate. I am, however, ready to conclude that in the Primitive African Tribes close to half-a million years ago and 50,000 YEARS AGO later in Australia, THE NATURAL CONSEQUENCES WERE ALMOST SIMILAR THAT THE SO-CALLED PRIMITIVE RELIGONS STARTED AND ARE STILL BEING FOLLOWED. It is a sad factor the term "Primitive" is not mentioned because of it negative connotation.

THE USE OF SYMBOLISM

I have always believed in Symbolism which played a very important role in all our Civilizations and unfortunately, very few people understood their important role BUT THESE TRIBES DID know and used it to the fullest extent. This is simply because the Symbolism is common for all religions and involves the CREATIVE IMAGES and symbols to represent the supernatural **Beings andIdeas.**Since I think, the Supernatural beings violate the principles of the NATURAL WORLD, there will always be difficulty in communicating and sharing supernatural concepts with others. I think, this can be overcome by anchoring these supernatural beings in material form by association with DRAWINGS AND ART, both practiced by the Primitive Africans and the Aborigines. BOTH BELIEVE AND SO DO I THAT THE SUPER-NATURALS BEING IN MATERIAL

FORM BECOME EASIER TO COMMUNICATE. Some of the earlier evidence of symbolic behavior is associated with the Middle Ages in Africa. Since 100,000 years ago, the researchers found the use of pigments such as red ochre and apparently, were used for ritual purposes.(Reference : Jared Dymond -guns, germs and steal — Published by NY Norton -page 277, 1997)

INVENTION OF WRITING: Following the Neolithic revolution, the pace of cultural evolution increased its pace after invention of writing during 5000 years ago. SYMBOLS THAT BECAME WORDS WERE THE EFFECTIVE METHODS OF COMMUNICATION. In those times, religious ideas mark the beginning of religious history. THE CLASSIC CASE OF EFFECT OF WRITING WAS IN ANCIENT INDIA WHEN THE CUSHITES WERE IN INDIA 100,000 YEARS AGO. I BELIEVE, **THEY PERFORMED THE PRIMITIVE RELIGION IN INDIA ALSO AND ONLY WHEN THE WRITING WAS INVEWNTED IN INDIA 5000 YEARS AGO, THESE ILITERATE CUSHITES WROTE THE FIRST VEDAS. I SINCERELY BELIEVE THIS IS THE FIRST TIME THESE FACTS ABOUT A RELIGION ARE SPELLED OUT IN DETAIL.**

IN CONCLUSION, THE PRIMITIVE RELIGION INVENTED IN AFRICA AND FOLLOWED SUBSQEUNTLY IN AUSTRALIA WERE ESSENTIALLY SIMILAR IN NATURE AND ITS THEOLOGY. I BELIEVE THIS RELIGON WAS ALSO IN INDIA 10,000 YEARS AGO AND MADE A DRAMATIC CHANGE AFTER THE INVENTION OF WRITING 5000 YEARS AGO.

THIS WAS THE BEGINNING OF OTHER RELIGIONS THAT FOLLOWED.

THERE ARE MANY OTHER FACETS OF PRIMITIVE RELIGION THAT HAVE DEFINED OUR PRESENT CULTURE AND THE VERY ESSENCE OF HUMAN BEINGS. IT IS UNFORTUNATE THAT THE NAME

"PRIMITIVE RELIGION" HAS LITERALLY DONE MORE HARM TO ITS PROGRESS AND ITS TRUE IDENTITY. I WILL TRY TO COVER MANY ASPECTS TO BRING THE PRIMITIVE RELIGION TO ITS PRE-EMINENCE.

PART - 7

PRIMITIVE RELIGIONS

EVOLUTIONARY FORMS OF RELIGION - SECTION 3

As you well know after reading my recent articles, the name Primitive Religions is a name given to religious and traditional beliefs in ancient Africa. Their practices of those old cultures were developed in societies which had not developed sophistication and hence, THE Western Civilization called these religious beliefs "PRIMITIVE" or "PRIMAL". I believe these terms are absolutely wrong and it was total ignorance of the sophisticated Western historians and lack of knowledge and understanding which caused this problem. THIS IS ANOTHER EXAMPLE OF WESTERN NAÏVE APPROACH TO NON-WHITE CULTURES AND TRADITIONS.

This article is presented here as a summary of my previous articles and the main purpose is comparison of all religions and relate where the Primitive Religion belongs.

INTRODUCTION

1. This Primitive Religion is the belief and practices who lack any religious books because the writing was not invented but the Religion noOt only existed but spread all over the vast African Continent.

2. This religion is without Divine guidance, trying to make its PEACE with the powers of NATURE.
3. The Primitive man may lay bare the basic character of all Men simply because he is stripped of the Material benefits that mask our need for God.
4. I believe this religion was practiced heavily in its pure form among the pre-literate people who practiced primitive thoughts and practice to varying degrees.
5. In the past few years, there is growing understanding of the "Mysterious" Eastern and African religions.

CONCEPT OF GOD

6. The Native Africans believe in a large number of Gods, each reigning over family, clan, village or some localities. This belief is called "HENOTHEISM" which means close adherence to a certain God while recognizing the existence of others.
7. Most of these religions believe in ONE SUPREME HIGH GOD who is their first source of existence.
8. Some also believe in many local Gods who are generally lacking in mercy and love.
9. The gods are not connected with their Dead Ancestors. God relates to their tribe, the customs and keeps the group functioning well.

MAN AND UNIVERSE

10. Aborigines believe the Gods are in total control of the Universe.
11. Droughts, illnesses and death pose threats to primitive man and his religion provides him a security of security.
12. It is thought that Ancestors and Gods control Human Destiny, handling out rewards and punishment for actions that may hinder or help the group.

13. I believe, like BUDDHISM AND HINDUISM BUT UNLIKE CHRISTIANITY, THE PRIMITIVE WORLD IS CYCLICAL. THERE IS NO PURPOSE TO HISTORY. VARIOUS AGE GROUPS REPEAT THEMSELVES WITH NO FINAL GOAL. (OBSERVATIONS FROM THEIR MURAL PAINTINGS)

SALVATION AND THE AFTERLIFE

14. All primitive religions believe **that one day, Messiah will come one day and bring in a reign of PEACE and PROSPERITY.**
15. In the next life, man is expected to merge with his ancestors in another world. These tribes NEVER described the NEXT WORLD.
16. Salvation is piecemeal, relating to worldly distresses. Sacrifice –most often blood sacrifice of animals is the usual means of atonement.
17. Temporary relief into the Realm of **"SACRED TIME"** or **"DREAMTIME"** are possible. Mythological stories are plentiful in their social lives.

MORALS

18. Survival is most IMPORTANT. The entire Society has very strict codes of conduct and everybody is asked to participate in the rituals.
19. Lying, cheating, stealing and murder are forbidden.
20. Primitive morality is thus a matter of transactions, of acting in ways that will benefit the society.

WORSHIP

21. When people gather, the Head of that group is called "A HOLY MAN" who regularly make journeys to the land of "GODS".

22. Use of TOTEMISM is common. Use of animals, plants and even human artifacts are common.
23. As they leave the prayer, people are given sweets and some water.

I found this article supplied by the Australian Government and find it very useful. This reminds me of the WORSHIPS, BELIEFS AND OTHR RELIGIOUS PRACTICES OF THE CUSHITES IN INDIA MORE THAT 100,000 YEARS AGO AND IT IS ALL SPELLED OUT IN DETAIL IN MY BOOKS ON HISTORY OF ANCIENT INDIA.

I AM VERY ELATED BY THIS DISCOVERY AND NOW AM CONVINCED THAT THESE ABORIGINES DID COME FROM INDIA AND STILL PRACTICE THE OLD CUSHITIC FORM OF RELIGION THEY BROUGHT FROM ETHIOPIA.

PART - 8

PRIMITIVE RELIGIONS

EVOLUTIONARY FORMS OF RELIGIONS—SECTION 4

In my eternal quest to find the true history of events in human lives, I came across this article in the New Scientist magazine of October 2005 and it dawned on me there are other fascinating factors on the subject of Brain Size and the birth of a religion and preference of our other animal species.

THE NEW SCIENTIST ARTICLE: (2005): This article on Elephants may pay homage to dead relatives written by S. Bhattacharya and it reads as : The elephants develop a strong preference towards an elephant skull (middle) rather than the skulls of a buffalo or a rhino. Apparently, elephants pay homage to the bones of dead relatives in their home ranges, a study of the animal's response s to skulls and ivory suggests. **Humans apart, only a few animals showany interest intheir own dead**. "But their interest in the ivory and skulls of their own species means that they would be highly likely to visit the bones of relatives who die within their home range". I do not have any scientific evidence on the effect of elephant's brain size and its other activities. But this amazing work has lot to tell us than I realized.

I was literally stunned by this article when I was in the middle of explaining my own hypothesis **on the RELATION**

OF A BRAIN SIZE of a human related to the ORIGIN OF RELIGION IN **THE COURSE OF HUMAN HISTORY.**

SOCIAL BRAIN HYPOTHESIS

According to Professor Dunbar, by 2.4 million years ago, Homo Habilis had appeared in East Africa, the first known human species. About 200,000 years ago, Asia and Europe were colonized by Neanderthal people who were extinct by 40,000 years ago followed by appearance of modern human beings.

(Reference: Dunbar, R.P.I 1998: The Social Brain hypothesis. pages 178- 190. Proceedings of the Royal Society 2014) .

About 80,000 years ago, three main lines of Homo Sapiens diverged and this was based on DNA classification. "The great leap forward" leading to full behavioral modernity sets in the separation and the migration of the Species started from Africa followed.

Prof. Dunbar's thesis argues that human intelligence did not evolve primarily as a means to solve ecological problems but as a means of Surviving and reproducing **in large and complex social groups. The dynamics of these groups relate to the "THEORY OF MIND" or** the ability to understand the Thoughts and Emotions of others. Dunbar and his co-workers further argued that when the size of the social groups increases, the number of different relationships grows by orders of magnitude.

In human's mysterious journey to become Intelligent, **Socializing Creatures like Human Beings innovated an essential order role of RELIGION**. "You spread something quite literally to stop everybody from killing everybody else out of just crossness" said Dunbar. "Somehow, it is clear that religions, all these doctrinal religions,

CREATE THE SENSE THAT WE ARE ALL ONE FAMILY.

I find this personally a very profound way of understanding the beginning of the concept of a **"RELIGION". How True!**

Humans, Dunbar found are capable of maintaining significantly more social ties than the size of our BRAINS alone could explain. I believe, each human being is surprisingly consistent in the number of societies. Therefore, RELIGION includes numerous elements of human social lives. **REPETITIVE CHANTING ARE COMMON IN ALL RELIGIONS. PRAYER BEADS IS ANOTHER GOOD EXAMPLE**. EMOTIONAL STORIES (MYTHOLOGICAL) IS ANOTHER GOOD EXAMPLE. **"What you get from singing on its own is its SENSE OF BELONGING. All these happen very** quickly. **According to some psychologists in Dunbar's group, that this can trigger very easily TRANCE STATE. Personally, I find this so amazing that I cannot describe the joy of reading and narrating to all of you.**

In my personal life, I came across few very religious people of different religions and the above description fits all of them. I AM AMAZED AT DUNBAR AND HIS GROUP'S PIONEERING AND BRILLIANT WORK. **The birth of a** religion and its basic **concepts always intrigued me but did not have any data to support my claims until I read Dunbar's work.**I support his work entirely and hope somebody should carry on this work. I wonder whether there is a hypothesis where differences between different religions and the brain size or any other factor.

TIMELINE OF HUMAN BRAIN SIZE

1. 6.2 MILLION YEARS AGO:

(A) Early humans begin to walk upright B) Brain size increases

2. 2 MILLION YEARS AGO -800,000 years ago C) Early humans spread around the globe, encountering many new environments in different countries. Following is the illustration of brain size with human history. Just to remind all: WE ARE HOMO-SAPIENS.

FIGURE - 1

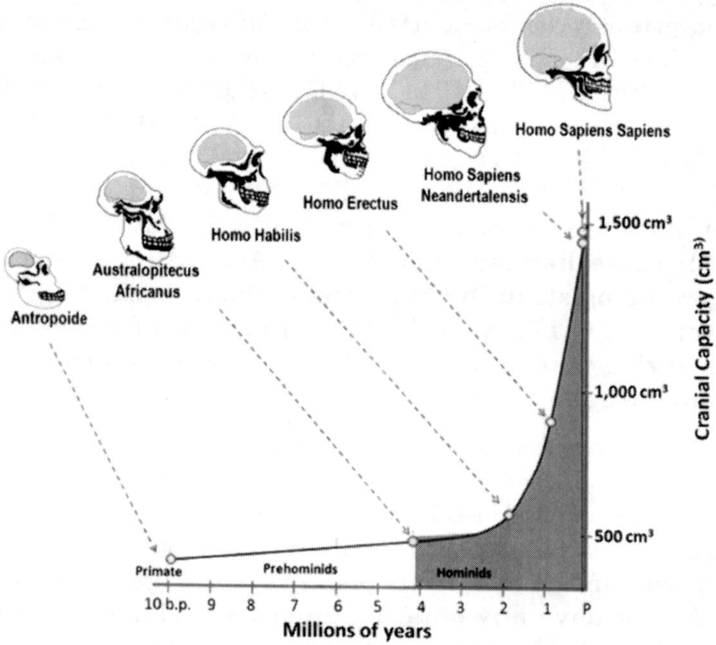

Figure: BRAIN SIZE HAS SIGNIFICANTLY INCREASED WITH AGE

d. FROM 800,000 YEARS AGO TO 50,000 YEARS AGO For some reason, there was a very high increase in MENTAL **CAPACITY from 50,000 years TODATE.**

FIGURE - 2

Figure of BRAIN SIZE WITH THE DEVELOPMENT OF HUMAN CULTURE

(Both these figures come from the work of Patricio Diaz:

Ref.bys.con@gmail.com. FIGURE 3

RELATIONSHIP BETWEEN AN INDIVIDUAL AND A GROUP WITH THE NATURE

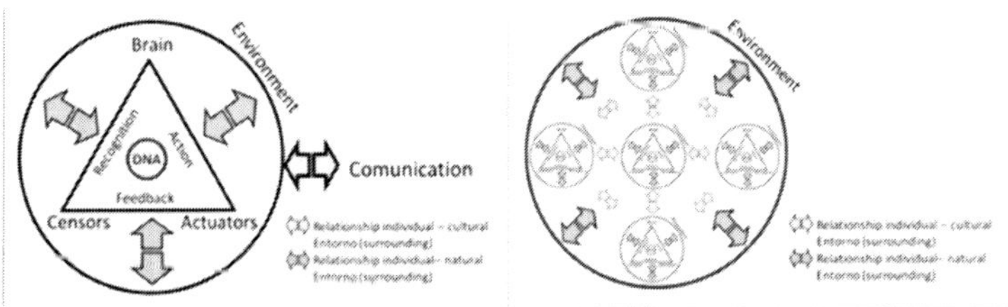

The evidence presented here has many effects on Human Culture such as

1. COMMUNICATION: FIGURE 4

2. RELIGION: Marcel Eliade's phenomenal work on the perceptions of the SACRED where the religious sentiments is characterized by a FEELING OF SMALLNESS COMPARED TO THE NATURAL FORCES ON THE GREATNESS OF CREATION.

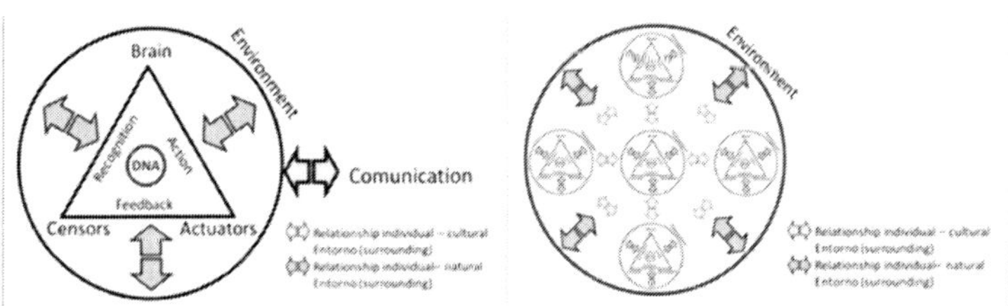

TIMELINE OF WORLD'S RELIGIONS :(These are my collected data)

1. 500,000 years to 5,0,000 years ago –Primitive religion
2. 50,000 years to 10,000 years ago - Primitive religion, Birth of democracy, Beginning of farming, husbandry etc.
3. 10,000 years to 4000 years ago - Still Primitive religion followed by advances in language from symbolism, writing, mathematics etc.

   Writing of VEDAS in India— Beginning of VEDISM as a religion.
4. 4000 years to 1000 years ago - Buddhism, followed by Hinduism, Christianity.
5. 500 A.D. Birth of Islam

I WOULD LIKE MY READERS TO RELATE THE FIGURES 1 AND 2 WITH THE CHART SHOWN ABOVE AND YOU WILL NOTICE A REMARKABLE INCREASE IN RELIGIONS AS WE APPROACH TODATE. I HOPE MY CO-RELATION IS CORRECT AND AM GLAD TO HAVE CONRTIBUTED TO THIS SUBJECT.

CONCLUSIONS

In order to understand the role of RELIGION in the human evolution, we must look to the very origin of life. As I contemplate the past, the, most up-to- date technology today seems to be simply imitate the same basic methods we have inherited: **A SORT OF SURVIVAL KIT. RELIGION TENDS TO OFFER COMFORTS TO HUMAN BEINGS AND WE DO DESERVE THIS AS LIFE GETS MORE INVOLVED.**

References

1. Dunbar, R.: Grooming Gossips of the evolution of languages : 1996 Published by Faber and Faber.

2. Dunbar, R. Pearce, E, and Stringer, C.: New insights in brain organization—Proceedings of Royal Society -2013.
3. Eliade, M: 1958 Birth and rebirth Simon and Schuster.

PART - 9

PRIMITIVE RELIGIONS

RELATIONSHIP BETWEEN BRAIN SIZE, HUMAN ANTHROPOLOGICAL BACKGROUND AND RELIGION - ARE THEY RELATED?

In my earlier articles, three important factors such as the Brain Size of a Human, the social evolutions of Humans and the religion prevalent at that time among its people and its inter-relationship can be described as:

Paleontological facts Brain Size Religion

1 million years ago very small No

0.5 million years ago growing Primitive

100,000 years ago growing Primitive

50,000 years ago growing Primitive

100,000 years ago still growing Primitive

50,000 years ago still growing Primitive

10,000 years ago Fully grown Advanced activity

Symbols, mythology

5,000 years ago Fully grown Writing invented

First writing ;religious texts

2000-1500 years ago Fully Grown Five major religions

(All references are spelled out in my earlier articles).

There are many legitimate questions arising out of these data and how to interpret the right way. I will start with the Primary religion which is the basic of all religions which may answer many questions.

PRIMITIVE RELIGION

I believe we have now established the Religious Beliefs of the Primitive Religion, often isolated, preliterate cultures which have developed sophistication of a society. This religion of archaic cultures –the cultures of the Paleolithic, Mesolithic and Neolithic ages (200,000 to 80,000 years ago) are also referred to as Primitive. (Personally, the Term **PRIMITIVE is absurd because there is nothing primitive about this religion**. From my knowledge of other religions, I personally consider the precepts of the Primitive religion are equal to or even superior to other religions).

An intellectual-Rational Report on the Primitive Religion is exemplified by the famous French Religious expert, Emile Duckheimer who saw Religion as the deification of the Society with structures. He believes in "Collective Representation" of the social sphere and ritual function to unite the INDIVIDUAL with the SOCIETY. In my opinion, there are three basic reasons why, I think, the Primitive Religion is a Superior Religion.

1. Primitive Religion started as a revolutionary form of religious life.
2. The other religions which followed in the past 1000 years were derived from the basic concepts of the Primitive Religion, all of it from the Nature and that is the main Reason that religion went all the way to the Australian Aborigines thousands of miles away and thousands of years later.

3. This Primitive Religion, in my opinion, **expresses a doctrine of reincarnation and implies that the Soul is a portion of the Totemic Principle.**

Once again, I am venturing into an abstract topic and that is the Primitive Religion is the. **PRECURSOR of OTHER RELIGIONS SUCH AS BUDDHISM, HINDUISM AND CHRISTIANITY**

An expert, MirceaEliade expressed has expressed that the Primitive Religion and Primitive Cultures are OPEN to the World of Natural Forms. This openness allows them to the World of Natural Forms which allows the people to experience the World as a Social Reality and the theory of reveling of the sacred is a TOTAL EXPERIENCE. This definition fits in properly with Durkheim's definition "A religion is a system of beliefs and practices relative to Sacred Things, that is to say, things are set apart and forbidden beliefs and practices which unite into one Simple Moral Community called a temple or a church.

CONCLUSIONS

Primitive Religion is the Beliefs and practices of people who lack writing and have a simple, material culture.

It is the Religion of Man without Divine Guidance, trying to make his Peace with the Mysterious Powers of NATURE. It can be said that the lays bare in the BASIC

PART - 10

PRIMITIVE RELIGIONS

Preface: Since my adventure to understand the Australian Primitive religion and subsequently, the main African Primitive religion in my last few articles, many main questions have remained unanswered and now, I would like to address them:

First was the reason for A RELIGION for all the humans. Can this be accomplished? This attempt to have a world religion for everybody has failed all these years. Can this effort be revived?

Second was, what was wrong with the Primitive religion to form new religions in the last thousand years. The enlarged human brain is one of the answers.

Third was, how do these new religions compare with the oldest one? Are there any similarities to begin with or are they diametrically opposite?

Most of the following information comes from various scholars known for their theological expertise and I tend to agree with some of their conclusions.

In all sincerity, I would like to know if there was anything wrong in the Primitive religious aspects which was necessary to establish other religions.

TITLE: RELIGIONS EVOLVE FROM PREVIOUS RELIGIONS — PART 1

(From Voltaire: "In metaphysics, in moral philosophy, the ancients have said everything. We coincide with them or we repeat them)."

While Theology is an ancient intellectual discipline, no one can doubt the momentous special significance of Religion around the World in human history. Study of the subject provides us an understanding of the intellectual underpinning of religious traditions and of the social and cultural contexts for religious beliefs and practices. This deep tradition of a religion has never been disputed in the human history.

If there is one term which is, consistently identified with anthropology all over the world, it is "Primitive Science, primitive religion, primitive peoples etc. According to the dictionary, the term "Primitive" is defined as "Pertaining to the beginning as original or in early times". Religious freedom, both as a term and as an ideal is a staple of modern liberal discourse. It is involved often in practical and legal discourses and in academic circles.

Although, all religions are seen as engines for the discovery of metaphysical strength, it could be maintained that at "Stake" in the promotion and protection of religion or belief is not so much of the search for one unique and exclusive truth but rather a search to promote greater respect for the rights of individuals, groups and communities.

It is clear that the major religions while concerned with the ultimate questions, such as Protectors and Promoters of Human dignity. They see themselves in particular **as defenders of the deprived and poor. So their religious freedoms is a freedom in a society not merely to believe** and worship but also to uphold the course of the deprived.

Religions evolve over time. There are very few genuine new elements of relief as there are not reported from previous religious ideas, from our previous cultural symbols and beliefs or from secular innovations. Nearly every aspect of every world religion was inherited from the culture and beliefs that pre-dated it. Karen Armstrong, an expert on World religions(Author: A short history of Myth. The author states how old myths resurface in a disguised state. The best example I have is the myths of the old Mesopotamian civilization in 4000 B.C became partly Indian myths of 3000 B.C. and later Greek myths in 500 A.D.). In reality, these myths were repeated over the time and different countries. NEARLY ALL BELIEFS HAVE HISTORIES OLDER THAN THE RELIGION THAT PROCLAIM THEM. There are plenty of data to support this case.

EXPOSURE TO THE FIRST AUDIENCES

A religion or a sub-set of a religious ideas, is sometimes moved from one culture to another. The Theosophists brought Indian spirituality to the West, interpreting it through in Western formal framework and changing its main character. It took tremendous work by Swami Vivekanand to correct many mistakes(in the beginning of the 20^{th}century). For example, **The strict teacher student relationship, lifelong disciplines were de-emphasized in the West and the New Age.**

So religious beliefs and practices often appear NEW because fans have taken them from one part of the world to another, where they are unfamiliar. Once they are blossomed in a new location, they are re-interpreted according to the New Culture Host's pre-connection and philosophical histories. THIS INTERPLAY RESULTS IN RELIGION CONCEPTS IN AN AREAS SOMETIMES BECOMING SUSEQUENT TO NEW SOUNDING RELIGION.

VARIOUS LINKS

CULTURAL RELIGION VS. SCHOLARLY RELIGION

Sometimes, the impact of a Culture can cause entire religion in another in places like Australia and South America; primitive tribes have formed religious practices that anthropologists call "CARGO CULTS" where they do rituals and dances as if they are controlling ships on the horizon. This, I believe, is an expression of the Human Instinct to control the SPIRITS that inhabited everything but its expression has softened in accordance with contact with another culture.

IT IS MY BELIEF AND CONVICTION THAT ALL RELIGIONS WENT THROUGH A SIMILAR PROCESS. THERE IS NO EXCEPTION TO THIS. SOMETIMES, SPAWNING A COMBINATION OF ELEMENTS THAT BECOMES TO BE COMBINED IN A NEW RELIGION. The best example is conversion of Vedism to Buddhism and later to Hinduism.

PSYCHOLOGY OF EXAGGERATION

Stories have a way of becoming bloated and exaggerated and some theorize that this is the basis of religions in general. (I can recall many mythological stories from the Mesopotamian region with the similar stories from the Indus Valley to the Greek civilization – each claiming to be the original authors). There are many reasons for carrying out the show such as boasting, national pride, to claim race superiority etc. On the other side, there is also much unnecessary downgrading of some religions to show superiority. All these fictional stories should be avoided. Some of these stories need more attention than provided by historians. These stories were written with a strong purpose such as national past-time and people's tales.

EVOLUTION OF FOLKLORE

The best example is the epic story of **GILGAMESH WRITTEN in** Mesopotamia in about 4000 years ago which was followed by Mahabharata and Ramayana between 3000 and 2500 years ago respectively. This was followed by the Greek poems, The Iliad and the Odyssey by Homer. Writing was invented and suddenly, the aspiration to write epics became pretty interesting and we witnessed the divine folklore from three separate areas.

I will continue with this subject in Part 2 of this article.

PART - 11

PRIMITIVE RELIGIONS

SUB-TITLE: A NEW RELIGION EVOLVES FROM OTHER RELIGIONS —PART 2

In the last Part, I discussed many important aspects of a need for a religion and what were the reasons for replacing the So-called Primitive or Primal Religion with the others that followed. Was there any obvious need for replacement and what really was the intention? In this article, I am expanding my RATIONALE TO INCLUDE OTHER factors that would answer our questions.

Given the documented facts that all present era religions have evolved from previous religions and beliefs, I am faced with the question "What causes the whole cycle; what is in our human brains which tends to believe in this way".

RELIGION INHERITED

In most countries on this Earth, most people use religion. The question is WHY? To me, the main reason is that children assume the Religion of their parents and they are unlikely to switch, or, if they do convert, it because a member of different religion in that family or some extraordinary reasons. According to David Myers, the famous religion expert (1999), the word Religion enters the index from the chapters on conformity and indoctrination: It is absolutely clear most religious people did not choose their religion nor have they seriously compared religions to ascertain which ones were most likely to ascertain which ones were most likely to be true. I Think, MOST PEOPLE CONFUSE THEIR HERITAGE FOR THEIR RELIGION. There is plenty of TRUTH in this statement. PEOPLE DO NOT THINK **BUT THEY ACCEPT RELIGION AS PART OF THEIR BIRTH RIGHTS.**

SOCIAL FUNCTIONS

Many people, I know fairly well, often adopt religious position for social reasons. Associating with a group of people of like-minded folk feels good and can engender a feeling of servers, a functional purpose quite separate from its actual religious contacts. Most of the people adhere to a religious life because it helps them to combat loneliness, helps them stay off alcohol etc. In the Western World, especially this country, some people join religion because "a Cohesive, supportive climate for a church which provides social networks". I find this movement encouraging since it draws people into a bigger crowd.

IS RELIGION ACTIVIST OR REACTIONARY ?

All the religions are associated with particular stances on the same subject. Women's human rights is a big issue from the late 19th century when alternate religions were strongly appealing or their stance on gender equality and these religions became magnets for feminists and activists. The issue of birth control drove many women from Catholicism to Protestant group. Although there were also some theological concerns, the mass of the movement was clearly socio-political in nature.

POLITICAL POWR STRUGGLE

According to Lester Kurtz (2007. God in global villages) Religion has traditionally been linked to special geographic locations in this world. Because Faith Traditions can either sustain or subvert the social system in these places, some traditions attract the system's elites. The best example is the adoption of ISIS in the Middle East where two countries have been totally destroyed. The leaders of the so-called religious group use religion as the symbol of unity and thus ruin everything.

Spain and Portugal took over all of South America and Roman Catholicism was installed as their religion. Spain did the same thing in Philippines and Catholicism was installed.

MORALIZING

Religions almost universally emphasize the moral duty of the individual. "God knows all" as all religions write repeatedly. We answer to God eventually. Buddhism and Hinduism teach that we pay tho consequence of this life throughout our next. So many people come to think of religions a being a bastion of moral thinking because, religions tend to dramatize and exaggerate the rewards and punishment of good and bad behavior. This emphasis is strong amongst lay people: despite their record against human rights as an institutional and national level. Local religions are seen as good religions, support morality. I do want to add the Simplicity and Drama of Religious stick and carrot approach to morality often makes religions appealing. The best example is the present Muslim problem of ISIS in the Middle East.

CULTURE AND MYTH

I always thought Myth and Religion are universally tied with Human Culture. In the last twenty or so odd years, they have become individual areas. Human experiences as narrated all over the World has changed the category completely. Agricultural people had Gods and rituals that waxed and waned, lived and died with the seasons as Native

Hunting Tribes had Gods and rituals that would secure their Luck in the hunt (Australian Aborigines is an excellent example). These Gods produce their environment and personal stories told about them as products of their imagination.

THE FEAR OF DEATH AND DESIRE —AFTER LIFE

Many people believe that religion provides reassurance against the specter of death. The thought of the permeant cessation is not a happy occasion, confusing and difficult to accept. Any theory that posits our ultimate survival can have a lot of appeal. There is an old Indian (Kushite phrase in the Vedas) **"Fear was the first thing on Earth to make Gods."** It also states that Vedism gives us a sense of power over death.

It is likely that one variable showing particular importance in protecting individuals from anxiety **about Death in the belief of After-life.** The stronger the belief, the less anxiety we have about DEATH. I strongly believe this was the MAIN BELIEF OF THE ORIGINAL INDIANS ROUND ABOUT IN 4000 B.C. AS THE WRITING DEVELOPED AND THE VEDAS WERE WRITTEN AND THIS WAS SPELLED OUT IN DEPTH.

CONCLUSION

You may or may not agree with some of my conclusion on this topic of Religion. While religious beliefs are the result of parental instructions and geographical incidence, there are many sub-conscious and other factors and superstitious beliefs that prosper. I CALL THIS IDEA OF FUNCTIONALISM WHEN RELIGIOUS LABELS OR REJECTING TYPICAL CULTURAL BEHAVIOR. THERE IS NO DOUBT THAT RELIGION IS MOSTLY CAUSED BY SOCIAL AND PSYCHOLOGICAL FACTORS AND NOT BY ANY EXAMINING OF THE EVIDENCE OR LOGIC BEHIND THE BELIEFS.

References

1. Karen Armstrong : (2005) A short history of myth. Vol.1 – Alfred Knopf publishers
2. Crabtree, Vexen(2002) Experience of GOD and Illusions (2002)
3. MirceaEliade:

PART - 12

PRIMITIVE RELIGIONS

SIMILARITIES IN PRIMITIVE RELIGION CONTINUING IN MODERN RELIGIONS

PREFACE: This article is written to confirm my sincere belief in Primitive Religion and its close similarity to other well –known religions practiced today and personally, I call the Primitive or Primal as our NEW AGE RELIGION

SIMILARITIES BETWEEN PRIMITIVE RELIGION AND ITS CONTINUANCE WITHMODERN RELIGIONS :

PART - 13

RETHINKING THE CONCEPT "PRIMITIVE" RELIGION

If there is one term which is consistently identified with anthropology, it is the word "Primitive", an adjective used to describe the data found by anthropologists all over the world. I am trying to find similarities in Primitive religion and seven or eight other religions followed from time of 3000 years to 1500 years ago in a very short time. Why did it take thousands of years to found some other religions? What did the new religions learn from the old one and use it in their religions, if any? These are profound questions and I do not have answers to some of the questions raised by experts. Time has taken its toll and we will never find the answers.

Let me define the Primitive Religion one more time. This religion is the belief and practices of people who lacked writing and had a simple material culture. This culture has existed since the beginning of Humankind. It is also a religion without Divine guidance, trying to make Peace with the terrifying and mysterious power of Nature. I can also add that the Primitive Religion lays bare the basic character of all humankind because the Man is stripped of the material benefits that offer the magic gift of our need for God. Furthermore, I also believe, most of the Human race through the ages has followed the basic tenets of the Primitive

Religion without acknowledging. Since this original religion has developed over every continent of the World among various peoples which had no contact with each other, **IT IS AMAZING THAT MANY BASIC SIMILARITIES EXIST.**

GOD

Primitive religion believes in a large entity and also many types of gods, each reigning over a family, clan, village. They also believe in one Supreme "High God" who happens to be the first source of all existence. Their gods are generally connected in some way with DEAD ANCESTORS. Perhaps, even today many people believe implicitly in paying homage to our ancestors. I see a lot of logic and understanding in that belief. As a matter of fact, there are some religions who have set aside a day or remembrance.

MAN AND THE UNIVERSE

These people believe that the Universe is in control of the gods. This belief is similar to Buddhism and Hinduism but unlike Christianity. Salvation an after-life is important in their lives. They believe a Messiah will come one day and bring Peace.

RELIGIOUS DIVERSITY

This is the fact that there are significant differences in religious beliefs and practices. People tend to focus their attention on this diversity to make their own religion in a very high standard. I have come to believe in the middle course approach and that means people need to pick the best points in each religion and make an attractive bundle for all to understand and eventually agree with broad principles.

PRIMITIVE RELIGION: THIS WORLD'S FIRST RELIGION?

In my limited knowledge on religions, I believe the Primitive religion shows me an essential and permanent aspect of Humanity. How can the crude cults of the tribes men in Africa and Australia tell us anything about religions far more advanced in VALUE, TRUTH AND DIVINITY.

The existence of religion in all of the World's societies is the result of the Process of DARWINIAN natural selection where religion is a set of beliefs made by elders to enforce the moral values necessary to preserve the society which exploits a BELIEF and SUPERNATURAL powers to enforce the rules. In a Primitive society religion was used to build its society capable enough bring about any changes.

However, in modern world, the deep set beliefs in Supernatural powers has led to more harm than good. This is simply because people are willing to fight and kill when science has reached level of high enough to refute or make obsolete the claims of supernatural powers on which these beliefs are based.

PART - 14

PICTORIAL ART IN AUSTRALIAN ABORIGINES WORLD

A recent article in the Manchester Guardian newspaper said the Primitive Art is the "most sincere form of Art there can be". I have been interested in Primitive Religion since my research in the Tribal African ancient religion and have been very keen to explore this unique religion and understand the collaboration between the ancient people and its Nature.

This photo shows the painting of Baime made by an unknown Wiradjuri In 'BAIME' CAVERNS.

This photo of Wandujina in the Wornumurra George in Western Australia.

EARLY COMMUNICATION METHODS

Communications have existed in various forms since man appeared on Earth. The methods, however, consisted of a disorganized set of signs that could have different meanings to each human being then. I believe it was not until 0.5 million years ago after appearance of Homo Sapiens that communications began to take an international flavor. The most well-known form of Primitive Communication is CAVE PAINTINGS. This unusual artistic endeavor was created by a species of MAN that appeared around 300,000 years ago. The methods involved creating pigments made from juices of fruits and berries, colored minerals, animal blood. These pigments were used as to create depiction of primitive life on the caves and other flat surfaces. The main purpose of these early paintings has been debated for years but the most popular theory states that the depictions were used as a manual for others what animals are safe to eat.

Story telling came later to pass on information from one generation to generation.

SPIRIT COUNTRY — DRAWN BY A FEMALE ARTIST

Traditional owner groups including the KUKU YALANJI AND GNUGU YIMITHIR people in the BAMA REINFORCED group.

Performers play traditional music instruments, the Didgeridor and music sticks

I wonder if any of my readers can find whether these instruments were used in Ancient India at all.

CONCLUSION

As a student of Ancient Indian history, I research many avenues and various ways to discover something not reported elsewhere. The Australian Aborigines is such subject which is very exciting and revealing. These artists photos depict how ingenious these people were 50,000 years ago and totally cut-off from the rest of the world until recently. I am sorry I am not able to interpret these drawings and I urge some Indian art expert to step in and hopefully understand these valuable treasures for the country's benefit. One way to understand these drawings is to study similarity if any, between the famous Ajanta-Ellora caves drawings and other ancient cave or rock paintings.

PART - 15

THE PRIMITIVE RELIGION

A man's religion reflects his human need to feel at home in his universe and comfortable among his neighbors. Historically, he always sensed that he cannot stand alone ; that mysterious power in nature and society will not let him share but affect him at every step, he must be willing in harmony in either with them or with one originative being that has brought the whole world into being and in sovereign way, may command all its powers.

It so happens that the religions of the past few centuries have all reflected the human needs and concerns. The Neanderthals Man and his challenging successors, the Cro-Magnon men of France, Spain and Africa sought out good relations with no-human paves that pervaded as natural and affected human destiny.

PRIMITIVE RELIGION

Often the Primitive religions teach that a Messiah will come someday and bring in a Religion of Peace. There is little belief towards the Next of Life simply because a Primitive man expects to merge with his ancestors in another world when he dies.

Salvation is piecemeal, relating to specific world distress. It is not felt that the state of grace can be reached in any other formal way. Temporary escapes into the realm of "Sacred Time" or Dream Time are possible. Mythologies are used to participate mystically in the actions of Gods.

Morals: Survival of the group is of paramount importance. Without the use of Police, ways must be found to make good members adhere strictly to codes of conduct. The primitive world has developed communal ways of coping with the world.

This religion is the beliefs and practices of people who lack writing and have simply material culture. It also happens to be religion of Man without Divine Guidance trying to make peace with the terrifying and mysterious powers of Nature. It is possible that the Primitive man lays bare in the basic character of humanity because he is stripped of the material benefits that often mark our need of God.

Many of us have followed the Primitive Religion without even knowing or acknowledging the basic facts. Most of the Human Race has followed the Primitive Religion and we do not even know about it.

GODS: Most Primitive people believe in many Gods and reigning over a family, clan, village. That belief is called "HEMOTHEISM" which means close adherence to a certain God while recognizing the existence of others.

MORALS: Survival of the groups was of paramount interest. Without use of police, ways must be found to make members adhere strictly to the codes of conduct. The Primitive World has developed communal ways of coping with the world. Primitive morality is largely a matter of transaction, acting in ways that will benefit the self and the community.

WORSHIP: It has the purpose of binding community together, if giving them a sense of common purpose. Fasting, self-mortification and drugs are used to attain a state of Trance. The main purpose is to obtain communication from the world of Spirits and AT TIMES, PARTICIPATE THE LIFE OF GOD.

Please this article since my subsequent article will try to explain how did the Aborigines learn about their ancestral skills without even knowing THEM.

PART - 16

HOW DID THE AUSTRALIAN ABORIGINES LEARN THEIR CRAFT FROM THEIR ANCESTORS

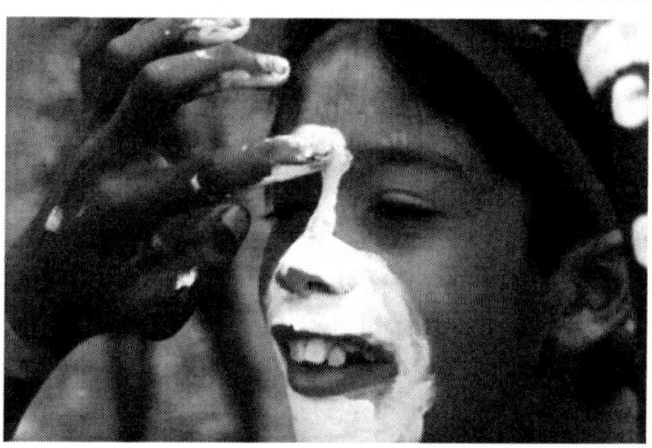

Aborigine Cave art -top picture, An young girl getting painted for some festival.

Archaeologists believe that the Aborigines came to Australia around 45,000 years ago. The aborigines, themselves, trace their ancestry to the CREATION BACK TO DREAMTIME, an era long past when the Earth was first formed. One Aborigine explained it this way: By dreaming, we mean the belief that long ago, these creatures started human society, they made all natural things and put them in a special place. Those dreaming creations were connected to a special place and special roads or tracks.

Apart from these HYYPERBOLIC statements, the TRUTH is quite different. As I stated earlier, these people went there from South India and **the BIG QUESTION IS HOW DID THEY LEARN SKILLS FROM THEIR ANCESTORS, WHOM THEY HARDLY KNEW.THEIR BACKGROUND WAS TOTALLY BLANK.**

In the past few weeks, I went through a huge list of articles and there was not a single reference to my question. WHY THIS HAPPENED and how did it escape the attention of very inquisitive British researchers. The true reason happens to be these Aborigines were not considered HUMANS and the government totally disregarded them for over 150 years. This is truly a shame on Humanity where such a utter disrespect for fellow human beings who were totally abused for such a long time. What should one expect from a former penal colony, lots of aggressive reforms and big plans to change mankind. The truth of the matter is that Australia is a white colony and will remain the bastion of white supremacy. Any other pretense is shear hypocrisy at its worst.

In this meantime, the Aborigines managed to survive by managing their environment very carefully while the Australian government spent millions of dollars telling the world how MAGNIFICENT they are towards the Aborigines. A TOTAL LIE AND THEY DID IT SKILFULLY.

This subject is very complicated since so much is unknown and a good deal is pure fantasy. It is very difficult to decipher and straighten out a lot of confusion. There were many times I simply gave up because truth was difficult to establish.

I am trying to solve this puzzle in my own way. Through the entire history, Humanity Hs always followed its own ancestral ways and passed it their next generation. In the case of the Aborigines, nearly 40,000 years have passed between the first generation to the present hundreds of years later and it was difficult to connect between the two generations.

The following article is my own CREATION, totally out of my knowledge of Ancient Indian History datingback 125,000 years ago. I wrote this history when I discovered the Ethiopians migrating to North India by land and to Kerala and Malabar area on the west coast of South India by boats. These unusual people called Kushites were extraordinarily clever people. They were nomadic people but since coming to India, a fertile land, they became bound to the earth and learned all the basic skill of gardening first, followed by farming and letting cattle grow on their land. If you have read my earlier articles, these people were unique since they were friendly and knowledgeable. Every evening they would meet after heavy work on farming during the day and all of that village would meet in the evening to share their day's stories. Since there was no written language, they wrote Symbols on trees and thus everyone corresponded with one another. Since writing was invented in about 3000 B.C., these people wrote the first VEDIC STRUCTURE ever written by a man.

These people were highly disciplined as I described earlier and were meticulous in their expressions. Discipline amongst them was very strict and everybody followed without a second thought. These are the people who really cultivated the deep culture of India and glorified to the fullest extent and today, these PIONEERS are hardly recognized by the Indian Elites who have very little regard for these people. The English did know after the fall of Indus Valley Civilization amongst the ruins but some -how, nobody put two and two together to draw a COHESIVE PICTURE. This is the fault of our educational system where we do not apply our analytical thinking power and History gets forgotten. Indian's history background is poor and not analytical to understand and relate all the facts in a succinct manner.

To get back to my article, these were the people who lived in a tight community all their lives and followed strictly the rules and regulations of their societies. To add, these people were well disciplined and stuck to their leader in spite of all kinds of problems. These were the people who decided to migrate to Australia or some land for safety of their tribes. All of us have to remember that the discipline was the cornerstone of their society and today, apparently, **they are still well disciplined.**

HISTORY OF THESE ABORIGINES IN AUSTRALIA

I decided not to accept the written version of their accounts simply because the time these migrants arrived was about 40,000 years ago and their version to English historians was in the late 17th and early 18th centuries. Almost many generations have passed among the Aborigines in that time and I believe, their version of history is anybody's guess.

Therefore, I decided to study their present day culture and draw subsequent conclusions from that research.Hope my approach is correct.

INTRODUCTION

The original inhabitants of the Continent of Australia took up residence at least 45,000 years ago before the Europeans landed in Brittany in 1788. That year, they were the majority, numbering around 300,000. In the late 1990's they became a minority struggling to claim rights in their traditional lands. Today, there is a great deal of resentment on the part of aborigines people for the treatment their ancestors received from their government. The Australian government literally spent millions of dollars on the new entrants from Europe rather than spend it on their own population.

LOCATION: The Aborigines traditionally lived through Australia and Tasmania. In the Central and Western desert regions, the aborigines were nomadic hunters and gatherers. They had no permanent place and residence, although they did have territories and ate whatever they could find and catch.

LANGUAGES

There are about 300 different languages spoken in 1788. Now, there are only 75. Some of these like **WALPIRI** are well established and no way of being lost. Their languages are taught in the aborigines schools.

FOLKLANE

Over their long history, a complex and rich abrasive mythology has evolved and it has been passed on for generations. This mythology is known as the "DREAMTIME" legends. This Dreamtime is the mystical time during which their Aboriginal Ancestors established themselves in the new land. Today, these myths are accepted as the CULTURAL LIFE of the people. I hope to find these stories and will write about them. Incidentally, mythology came very easy to these Kushites back in India and they invented Indian mythology which brought unbelievable stories together. These stories were later copied by the Persians and the Greeks. These Indian stories are fabulous in their contents and more I read them, more fascinated I get by its wisdom, caricature and dreamy thoughts.

RELIGION

Traditional aborigines revolve round the Dreamtime. Totems are also important part of their religious identity. Totems are symbols from their natural world (I believe, this is similar to their original assembly meeting every evening and carry a symbols who they are — This was old Kushite gathering format that took place every evening and each member took a small gift a leaf or a flower with him to their meeting.

The religious world is inhabited by the ghosts of the dead, as well as a variety of spirits who control certain aspects of the Natural World, such as Rainbow serpent who brings in rain. Ritual are used to placate these high spirits.

Incidentally, the African tribes back in the middle ages, also believed absolutely in their dead ancestors and copied them as many times a day. I believe this ritual is performed out of their loneliness of their lives in huge wilderness. There was no other escape but everyone went through without any second thoughts. The aborigines were not any different from their cousins in Africa and the rituals are similar in their nature.

We humans are supposed to live in societies, free of fear and in safety.

RITES OF PASSAGE

In their societies, there were both male and female rituals that mark the passage from childhood to adulthood. Death in their societies was accompanied by complex rituals. In some tribes, a wife would have to isolate herself from the rest of the society upon the death of her husband. (Very similar to the Hindu Society) She would live in a widow's camp for a period of three years. During that time, she would communicate only by a sign language. She was not permitted to speak. If a widow does not follow her tradition, her husband's soul could steal her soul which could lead her to death. It is unfortunate to read these Aborigines followed the similar traditions of their ancestors in India where a male was more important than a female and rules were followed accordingly.

RELATIONSHIP

Behavior and interpersonal relationship among these people is defined by FAMILY ROLES. In many societies, certain kinfolk stand in what are called "AVOIDANCE RELATIONSHIP WITH EACH OTHER". For instance, in some groups son-in-law avoids his mother-in-law completely. In other societies, son-in-law could only talk to his mother-in-law by a sign language. Incidentally, as I understand, these rules are strictly followed by younger generation.

Some aborigines find it hard to say Thank You all the time. These people have a sign language and they use it frequently.

I have learned from many articles that the young aborigines copy each and every detail of their parental lives and live by that strict code. NO WONDER THEIR TRADITION CONTNUES.

FAMILY LIFE

A marriage in these societies is complicated according to European sources but not to Indian people. Their families go over the birthday charts for days and only if there is a good match, a marriage can be arranged. Normally, husbands are much older than their wives. Australians simply do not understand this ritual. There are some tribes where marriages are arranged at birth.

There is one notable exception from their forefathers. Their older generation was really very good in astronomy and astrology. I did not find that in today's generation. I also did not find a big interest in arithmetic, geometry and mathematics.

CULTURAL HERITAGE

We have to remember most these societies are still nomadic. Because of this, they do not value material life and objects. For some reasons, they also did not develop any musical instruments. One that is well-known is the "DIJERIDOR" a long tube made from a piece of wood that has been hllowed by the termites.

Dance is rarely performed and only at big ceremonies.

CRAFTS AND HOBBIES

Their craft has become extremely popular in the World Keeping their right to pursue their traditional ways of life is one of the biggest social problems facing these people. IT IS VERY UNFORTUNATE THAT THIS MINORITY IS TOTALLY OVERWHELMED BY A MAJORITY WHO SIMPLY DO NOT UNDERSTND THEM AND THUS THE ENTIRE TREATMENT IS DEPLORABLE.

I HOPE TO ADD ON WHEN I FIND SUITABLE MATERIAL.

References

1. Berndt R.M. and Berndt C.H. — the world of first Australians—Sydney 1964.
2. Hans Sencha Le Braun — The sacred art of the kiwi-islands —1995.

PART - 17

SPIRIT IS THE DRIVING FORCE OF THE BODY

Three events occurred in the past few days which helped me to write this article. The first one was reading a book "The seat of the soul" by Gary Zakov, New York Times best seller for some time. This is an outstanding book about the birth of new species and explains of human perceptions past the five senses such as values of harmony, co-operation, sharing and reverence for life. In short, it is about authentic power in the alignment of personality with the soul.

Here are the few details of the book: The invisible spirit is eternal. A person is made of Body, Mind, Intellect (Buddhist teaching) and Spirit (Atma- Hindu addition). All these are required for a man to function properly and lead a wholesome life. Therefore, there must be connected Divinity within (Higher self, self-realization, and Supreme God). Any disconnection from each other will lead to degradation of man to animal life (lower self) .The question is what is the relationship among the Body, the Mind and the Spirit? The working senses are said to be higher than the Body. The Mind is higher than the Senses. The Intellect is higher than the Mind but The Spirit is still higher than the Intellect (Bhagwat Geeta 3.42). Everything ends in the Spirit.

The second one was reading an essay on the mind/body movement in the British Nature magazine (1982) where it was reported that the mind/body movement come together at more or less the same time. In the 1950's, Elmer Green, the founder of the biofeedback company, journeyed to India(Dalai Lama's residence) to study the yogis and their capacity to reach profound levels of consciousness that was accompanied by a mastery over physiology previously unknown in the West. He sought to record the brain nerves of three Masters to see if Westerners could be trained to emulate these mental states and the physiological mastery that accompanied them.He came to the conclusion that it would take many more years of research before any Western person could possibly emulate the monks.

My third event was an article Included in the same journal. Professor Herbert Benson of Harvard University went to study the **Concept of Relaxation Response, a technique to Calm the Mind.** He stayed for two years with the monks to study each and every aspect of their daily routine. He recorded something very unusual. These monks were able to take sheets dipped in frozen water, wrap these sheets around their unclothed bodies and then dry the sheets by mentally raising their body temperatures. **Each monk, situated in a freezing environment, dried onesheet after another. AN ABSOLUTELY AMAZING FEAT ! The physiology of this mastery was accurately measured and recorded.** I was literallystunned by this story. I had never read that one can raise one's body temperature at will. This was truly astonishing and never expected the enormity of these results. It makes me very humble that my knowledge of the Human experiences is very limited. A pity!

The invisible spirit is eternal. A person is made of Body, Mind, Intellect (Buddhist Teaching) and Spirit (Atma – Hindu addition). All these are required for a man to function The properly to lead a wholesome life. Therefore, these must be connected with each other to experience Divinity within (Higher self, self-realization and Supreme God of life). Any domestic from each other will lead to degradation of a man to animal level (lower self). The big question is what is the relationship among Body, Mind and the Spirit? The Working senses are said to be higher than the Body; the Mind is higher than the Senses, the Intellect is higher than the Mind but the Spirit is higher than the Intellect (Bhagvad Gita 3.42)

THE ONENESS OF BODY AND MIND

Buddha regarded life as the Unity of the physical and spiritual entities. He viewed all things, whether material or spiritual, seen or unseen, as manifestations of the same Ultimate Universal Law or source of life. This happened to be the main principles of the foundation of their religiousprecepts.Furthermore, that the physical and spiritual aspects our lives are completely inseparable and are of equal importance.

Materialists claim that the physical or the material world which can be measured and touched is the only "REALITY" where some spiritual traditions see the physical as mere illusions -or something inherently corrupt which exists in order to be transcended and the spiritual as the ultimate Truth.

Buddha regards life as the UNITY of the physical and spiritual. It views all things regardless of the background. In the Rig-Veda it states firmly that a "Person can know another's mind by listening to his voice. This is because the physical aspect reveals the spiritual aspect. The physical and spiritual which are one in essence, manifest themselves as two distinct aspects."

A person's inner emotional state will be revealed in his or her personal appearance. The feelings of someone in a happy and optimistic mood can be read in their faces; there may even be a skip in their step. In contrast, the painful gait and drawn features of a person weighed down by suffering can communicate his or her inner torment even from a distance.

Our inner state also affects the physical functioning of our inner feelings. Mental or psychological stress has been linked to a range of illness from the skin disorder, allergies, asthma and ulcers. On the other hand, a positive determination to overcome illness can "inspire" our organs and even individual cells toward health.

Many have pointed out that "**When our determination changes, everything will begin to move in the direction we desire. The moment we resolve to bevictorious, every nerve and fiber in our being will immediately orient itself toward our success. On the other hand, if we think, this is never going to work out, then at that instant, every cell in our being will be deflated and give up the fight**".

TRUE HEALTH AND GENUINE HAPPINESS MUST ENCOMPASS BOTH THE PHYSICAL AND THE SPIRITUAL

Buddhism as preached in the Rigveda views living being together of what it terms the "Five Components". These are: the physical aspects of life and the senses, the perception, which integrates the impression received through the senses; conception, by which we form ideas about what we have perceived; volition, the will that acts on conception and consciousness, the function of discernment that supports the functioning of the other components.

Life is the force of energy that keeps these five components functioning together as a harmonious and integrated WHOLE.

CONCLUSIONS

This is a liberating concept as it means there is no need

to seek enlightenment outside ourselves or in a particular place. Wherever we are, in whatever circumstances, we can bring forth our innate feelings, thus transforming ourselves.

CAN WE REALLY ACCOMPLISH THIS?

PART - 18

THE ABORIGINES MYTHOLOGICAL STORIES——

THIS STORY IS ABOUT GOD

In Aborigines mythology, the Earth's surface was nothing but a vast, non-de script expanse of mud or clay. But that life less landscape changed when ancestral spirits rose from beneath the surface or descended from the sky and assumed the form of animals, plants and humans. They the journeyed across the Earth, changing it by shaping the mud into rivers, hills, islands and other features. The ancestral beings also gave birth to all living things – including humans to whom they gave language, knowledge and beliefs.

The aborigines believe that they are also direct descendants of their Spirit beings. To them, it is important to track the journey of their Creation that a man's mythological ancestors took through the World, which is called a Songline and to speak the languages and learn the music of their ancestors.

One story they wrote about the origin of the Sunrise. In the myth, the sky is originally covered the Earth like a blanket, blocking the light of the Sun and everyone crawled in darkness until the magpies took upon themselves to change the situation. The birds gathered long sticks and pushed against the sky, lifting up and then wedged rocks under the sticks to lift up even further.

Eventually, the sky split open and the first Sunrise appeared. The birds were overjoyed to see the light and feel the warmth of the Sun's heat that they burst like a joyful song- a habit birds follow every morning.

Another life long story told by the Yorta Yorta people explain the origins of the landscape and its colors. GANE, a Dreamtime being who was a great rianbow colored snake went out to look for a old woman who had become lost. As he followed the most left the old woman's Cane, his body pushed against the Earth, moved the soil and rocks, thus creating hills and valleys birds and other animals. Another mythicals being, Sprit called Biami called out to Gane, in a voice so loud that caused thunder and huge rainfall which filled everywhere with water and deep crevices in the Earth left by Gane's body which became a river that the Yorta Yorta people called a DUNGALE which today is known as Murrays' River.

THE SIMPLICITY OF THE MYTHICAL TALES IS STRIKING. THE USE OF NATURAL OBJECTS SUCH AS CLAY, MUD AND THE SKY WAS THEIR ENTIRE LIFE'S MOST MEMORABLE POSSESSIONS AND THEY LITERALLY THRIVED ON THESE SIMPLE OBJECTS.

I WILL TRY TO CATCH UP WITH OTHER STORIES IN THE NEAR FUTURE.

PART - 19

THE ABORIGINES MYTHOLOGICAL STORIES

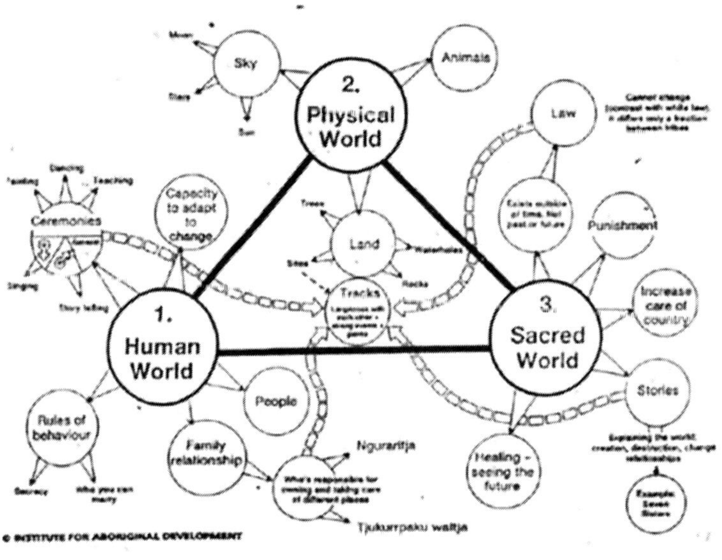

(The aborigines is a complex network of knowledge, faith and practice that derives from stories of creation which pervades all spiritual and physical aspects of their lives. This chart will provide a broad background to the width and depth of their stories. They do not have the deep penetration of the human psyche used in the Indian mythological stories but remembering their past, their effort is worth praising – DinuWagle)

The Aborigines speak of **JivaGurumwari, a seed power** deposited in the Earth. In their view, many meaningful activity, event or life process that occurs at a particular place leaves behind a vibration and residue in the Earth as plants leave an image of themselves as seeds. The shape of land, its mountains, rocks, riverbeds, and waterholes —and its unseen vibration echo the events that brought that place into Creation. Everything in the Natural World is the symbol of footprints of the metaphysical beings who action created our World. As with the seeds, the potency of an earthly location is wedded to the memory of its origin.

The Aborigines called this potency of the "Dreaming" of a place and the dreaming constitutes the Sacredness of the Earth. Only in extraordinary state of Consciousness can one be aware of the Earth. "Dreaming" is also often used to refer to as the individuals or groups set of beliefs or Spirituality. For instance, the Aborigine may also say that they have a kangaroo dreaming or shark Dreaming or any combination of Dreaming pertinent to their country.

Dreaming varies throughout the Country and there are different versions on the same story. For example, how the bids got their different colors when they are different in the North as in the South. In a complex network of knowledge, faith and practices that derives from stories of Creation which pervades all spiritual and physical aspects of Aborigine life.

They believe that every person is an essential way exists externally in the Dreaming. The external part of the Individual begins and continues to exist when the life of the individual ends. Both before and after life, it is believed that the Spirit –Child exists in the Dreaming and is only initiated into life by being through a mother. The Spirit of the child is culturally underwent to enter the developing fetus during the fourth month of pregnancy.

When the mother felt that the child moves in the womb for the first time, it was thought that the spirit of the land comes into effect and the and the child is considered the custodian of that part of the country. It was also believed that before animals, humans and plants came into being, their souls existed by themselves. Eventually, all the living beings become Guardians of the world.

PART - 20

DO YOU HAVE TO BE 'PRIMITIVE' TO FOLLOW "PRIMITIVE RELIGION"

This topic has been with me ever since I was surprised and elated when I read the elements of the Primitive Society. I was keen on knowing as much as possible about some of the religious aspects of this ancient religion.

Primitive Religion is a name given to religious beliefs and practices of these traditional, often isolated pre-literate cultures which have developed urban and technologically sophisticated forms of society. The term is awfully misleading and suggests that RELIGION is far less complex then the religion of "Advanced Societies". As a matter of fact, the other side of the argument is true. It is very unfortunate that every effort was made to increase the significance of the known religions at the expense of older ones.

Since the end of the 17th century, the Westerners began approaching the Asian and African countries to steal their natural wealth and conquer land to increase their growing empires. Initially, that country's religion did not come into picture but these foreigners found that some of the peoples they conquered followed a religion which they considered CRUDE and below a decent man's Christian religion and called the people **Primitive** and their religion **"PRIMITIVE".** These initial white colonialists were crude, hardly literate and degraded every- body who was not European with white skin. This was the beginning of the Christian church's missionary tours to convert as many natives to Christianity. Political power as usual was followed by the religious power significantly.

Only later in the 18th century, Oxford and Cambridge Universities took a lead and sent their paleontologists and experts to find more about the "Primitive Religion" and convinced themselves that this so-called Primitive Religion was more advanced, cultured than they earlier imagined. The pioneers amongst these pioneers were Sir James Frazer and Professor Taylor who made remarkable discoveries who studied studiously for decades and wrote remarkable books. But it was too late to change the original inappropriate word and this carries bad connotation even today. So much rubbish is written on this subject, it is not worth repeating it here. I am emphasizing more the true nature of this religion than many authors.

There are two main factors on this topic. Firstly, most of the people in the East, Africa and South America are religiously bound to their religion. Secondly, the White population of Europe does not simply understand this type of devotion by the non-whites and hence the bitterness towards the Primitive religion, The similar treatment by the British shown towards the Hindu and Buddhist religions through the British empire for 200 years. It is the absolute ignorance of other races, its philosophy, religion and social habits. This catastrophic approach has caused a lot of wars and killing of many people in the last few hundreds of years in Asia and Africa.

THEORIES OF PRIMITIVE RELIGION

This topic has moved between the two poles, one intellectual and rational developed on the North pole and the other Psychological and irrational from the South pole. Earlier anthropologists like Frazer and Taylor made few cardinal mistakes when they confused Subjective and Objective Realities in their belief that the Vital force (SOUL) is detachable and capable of independent existence. Many others including myself do not believe in BODY and SOUL are independent but are INSEPARABLE. These two English scholars had not studied the religious nature of depth and treated these two items totally separable.

Another religious approach by Professor Emile Durkheim who saw a Religion as the DEIFICATION of SOCIETY and STRUCTURE. The numbers of religion arise as the COLLECTIBLE REPRESENTATION OF THE SOCIAL SPHERE AND RITUAL FUNCTION TO WRITE THE INDIVIDUALS WITH SOCIETY. This pioneering thought was further expanded to articulate the way in which the structures of the Society are exemplified in Myths or Symbols. FOR THE FIRST TIME, THE EXTREME IMPORTANCE OF MYTHS, MYTHOLOGY AND SPIRITS AND SYMBOLS WAS UNDERSTOOD BY A WESTERN anthropologist. These European scholars read the so-called Greek mythological stories without understanding the REAL MEANING of the myths which originally came from India and was copied by the Greeks without knowing the meaning of it. It was Professor Durkheim who saw a new beginning of these mythological stories built in the Primitive Religions.

TO THIS WRITER, THIS WAS THE TURNING POINT OF A WESTERNER TOWARDS EASTERN RELIGIONS. FOR THAT MATTER, MANY EASTERNERS ALSO DO NOT UNDERSTAND THIS IS A BASIC PART OF THEIR RELIGION. THE ENTIRE EASTERN RELIGIONS LIKE BUDDHISM AND HINDUISM ARE WRITTEN AS A MYTHOLICAL TALES IN SYMBOLS AND SIGNS. THE VEDAS ARE ALL SYMBOLS AND ONE CAN DRAW DIFFERENT MEANINGS ON A BROAD SCALE.

To articulate this important argument, this pioneering thought was further expanded to include society structures as exemplified in Myths and Symbols. I can further argue that ALL OF US LIVE IN ONE UNIVERSAL FORM OF HUMAN LOGIC AND THAT THE DIFFRENCE THE THINKING OF PRIMITIVE AND MODERN PEOPLES CANNOT BE BASED ON DIFFERENT MODES OF THOUGHT OR LOGIC BUT RATHER THAN ON DIFFERNCES IN THE DAT ON WHICH LOGIC OPERATES.

EXPERIENCE AND EXPRESSION

Regardless of apparent psychological or intellectual is accepted, It is clear that the Primitives experience the World differently than do people in modern cultures. Intelligence has very little to do with it. Primitive thought is considered more concrete and this means the primitive experiences a different way of relating to objects and experiences of every -day life. I have personally experienced this difference in modern life but definitely cannot say the other guy is more intellectual than myself.

Another scholar, Marcel Eliade expressed a similar position. For him, primitive cultures was open to the world of Natural Forms. This openness allows them to express them experience than to Sacred Reality. In the Author's theory, the REVEALING OF THE SACRED is a TOTAL EXPERIENCE.

RITUALS

Many forms of Primitive Religion and cultures is expressed in Rituals and Ritualistic actions. The form and functions of these rituals are diverse and normally performed to ensure or to the favor of the Divine, to ward off evil or to make change in cultural status.

DIVINE BEINGS

These are usually known through the mode of manifestation. Creator-gods are usually Deities of the Sky who possesses an ultimate power. There is great similarity in forms between the Supreme sky deities of Primitive cultures. It is important to know that ALL THE PRIMITIVE RELIGIONS I AM FAMILIAR WITH HAVE MANY DEITIES IN THE SKY MORE THAN ANY KNOWN RELIGION.

Allied to and existing within the same sphere as the SKY –God and the manifestation of DIVINE presence in form of the SUN and the MOON. These DIETIES are creators by virtue of their growth producing powers where - as the SKY –GOD creates only ex-nihilists(out of nothing). They do not require human energy in this capacity.

The presence of the Moon is different from that of the Sun. Moon-deities are assimilated with a more rhythmic structure. They seem more vulnerable and more capable of loss and gain. Moon-deities are more often Female in form.

SUMMARY

Underlying all forms of functions, rituals and symbols in Primitive Religions is the distinction between the Sacred and the Profane. The Sacred defines the world of Reality which is the basis for all meaningful forms and behaviors in the Society. Profane has made a mode of existence and A QUASI- REALITY NOT BASED ON Divine Mode.

Regardless of our society, Primitive or modern, all of us two societies, the Sacred and The Profane. A mode of Ritual behavior defines our mode of Contact with the SACRED.

References

E. Durkheim : Elementary forms of Religion 1915.

Marcel Eliade : The sacred and the profane: 1959.

Part - 21

YOU CAN TAKE THE PERSON OUT OF THE PRIMITIVE AGE BUT NOT THE PRIMITIVENESS OUT OF THE PERSON

For the past fifty years, I try to keep abreast of the advancement in modern science, such as Evolutionary Psychology, sometimes called Modern Darwinism. I believe over the last few years, this evolutionary psychology as a discipline has gathered high momentum. A convergence of research and discoveries in genetics such as DNA reveal that human beings today inhabit a thoroughly modern world of space exploration. We do so with the ingrained mentality of stone-age hunter -gatherers. Homo sapiens emerged some 2,000,000 years ago but today, people still seek these traits that made survival possible over all these years. All of us have an instinct to fight furiously when threatened. I call the Human beings "Hard-wired" and it appears that we can take a person out of Primitive age but not the Primitiveness out of the Person. All of us can remove people out of their surroundings but we can do nothing to remove their Primitive behavior.

About 150 years ago, British Naturalist, Charles Darwin rattled the world with his theory of NATURAL SELECTION and accordingly human beings were not "placed" fully formed on the Earth. Instead, they were an " Evolved Species", the biological descendants of a line that stretched back to Ancient Simians. In fact, Darwin said, human beings shared a common heritage with all other species. I am a firm believer of this thesis.

Ever since Darwin, scientists have built with modern discoveries, most notably, in Genetics. We are now stating that "All living creatures" are designed by a specific contribution of genes. There is an environmental selection where some genes do not survive to reproduce. The genes that are surviving this rigorous selection are passed on to succeeding generation. We also have genetic mutation who have its own peculiarities. In this entire Evolutionary Process, **WE HAVE CREATED A HUMAN BRAIN IN OUR BODIES WHICH SHAPE OUR HUMAN MIND.** Over the last 50,000 years ago, a human being became so settled across the planet that we still hold on to what we learned in the Evolutionary Process.

THINKING AND FEELING

Ever since the beginning, the food supply and resources such as clothing, shelter were unreliable, bipeds like us strike us strength lay in our minds. The thought and emotions that have best served them were programmed into their psyches and continue to drive many aspects of Human Behavior Chief among these are:

(A) EMOTIONS BEFORE REASON

In this uncertain work, those of us who survived always had their emotional Radar turned on. I firmly believe that the **Primitive people came to trust their Instincts above all else.** This reliance saved lives and allowing who processed keep Instincts to reproduce. To me, Emotions are the FIRST SCREEN to all the information received.

(B) CONFIDENCE BEFORE REALISM

Recent data give us confidence that after terrifying conditions of the Stone age, those who survived surely were those who believed they would survive. Their confidence strengthened and attracted allies and brought them resources. These survivors passed on their genomes to their successors. Is it True that human beings put confidence before Realism and worked hard to shield themselves.

(C) CLASSIFICATION

I strongly believe the world of hunter-gatherers was very complex and constantly presented many problems. What to eat without poison, and therefore, humans developed enormous information and capabilities to eat only food that was healthy. Human beings learned to be judicious in their natural environment. Over confidence is a part of genetic legacy and there is a great prosperity to classify is we humans do not make it right. People are complex and many sided. But it is illuminating to know that we are programmed not to see them that way. But we have managed to survive.

(D) SKILL DEVELOPMENT

We have learned the Skill Development. If we went to develop someone's skills, the best way is to give them away our classifying situation. Our advanced math and science education today relies on sophisticated models of processes - a complex explanation of Cause and Effect in different circumstances.

(E) UNIQUE HUMAN NATURE

Along with the scarcity of food, clothing and shelter, the Stone – age also characterized our shifting social scene from one season to the next, it was not easy to predict who would have food to eat, let alone who would be healthy enough to endure the elements. In other words, our leaders who controlled other resources were always changing. Survivors were savvy enough to anticipate power shifts and adjust for them.

I have learned from the Revolutionary psychologists that our Primitive personality is so well adapted to precarious life of hunter-gatherers, will continue to call the tune whenever it is free to do so.

(F) ORGANIZATION DESIGN

Like the primates before us, Human beings were never loners. Indeed, the family is the center-piece of all human societies. Modern Darwinism thinkers hypothesize that humans survival was greatly helpful by monogamy – pair bonding was necessary for prolonged care of the young. And there was born the Clan or an extended family built through "marriage" that was very important.

Professor Dunbar of the Cambridge University and the University of Liverpool, U.K. found a linear relationship between the Brian Size of social primates. The larger size of the brain, the larger was the size of the Group. Unlike the animals, humans need social organization to survive and organize socially. These are held together by the bond of communities. It includes a lot of Brain Power – remembering people, forging alliances and keeping promises, etc.

CONCLUSIONS

If we study each of the Psychologist's, what can you make of this World? One can argue is to disagree on this process that is NURTURE and not NATURE, that makes who we are. Another route to consider the implication of evolutionary Psychology as you would consider a domestic problem.

References

Hill, P.A., Dunbar, R.I. — Social network size in humans –Human Nature 14, 53-72, 2003.

PART - 22

THE SHAPE OF THINGS TO COME – VISIONS FOR THE FUTURE OF ABORIGINES

In 2011, the Lowitja Institute (a private Australian Research Institute) embarked on research project using future thinking to consider how research might contribute to Aborigines welfare to the year 2030. Future Thinking is not about Research and management –is not about predicting future but rather about identifying a number of a plausible future and possible futures. It differs from traditional research methods in that it draws on deeper intuitive insights as well as hard evidence.

Work shops were held nationally to consider possible scenarios based on divergent futures: a Vibrant Australia in which the Aboriginal values are considered important and embraced as Central to Australian identity; an Australia in which economic and spiritual poverty drive a rejection of diversity and increase the Divide between the Rich and The Poor.

The Response was enormous and participants articulated a strong and widely shared for a profoundly different system in which research and practice, are closely inter-woven which enables greater integration of services but also be responsive to changing research demands. This was really a tall order where many things could not possibly be achieved well.

Consultation also identified an urgent need to address a social part of their Health problems.

Finally, the project identified the Aborigines Health and Poverty problems are its worst problems. Their conclusion is to request the Federal Government to spend more on health and finding ways to employ the population.

ABORIGINES HOLD THE KEY TO THEIR FUTURE

Since I live in U.S. for the past sixty years and saw a tremendous progress made by Non-whites and Hispanic communities, I am encouraged to assert that a similar progress could be made by the Aborigines in Australia. However, the problems with the Indigenous Affairs policy are fiendishly complicated. These days, as I understand, they are often the part of failed past attempts to improve the lot of these citizens as they are a result of Pure Racism. Whatever their source, they combine to condemn most of these original natives to sub-standard living. On almost every measure-health, schooling, housing, income, crime and incarceration- Aborigines Australians trails non-Aborigine Australians. The closing the gap strategy appears to have stalled. The last report showed progress on only two of the strategy's seven goals.

Attention has shifted a great national project to empower Aboriginal people-recognition in some form of the Constitution. The aim is worthy but fraught with difficulty and danger. This was described by an Australian Constitution expert is similar to Apollo 13 astronauts entering the Earth's atmosphere: the approach has to be just right. Too steep sand the craft will burn.; too shallow and it will skip off into space and be lost. Those framing a question to be put to a referendum must steer a course between seeking too much – and offending the constitutional conservatives which would see the proposal rejected. And seeking empty words which change nothing. Failure to pass a proposed amendment, most agree, would be disastrous.

Given the history of Constitutional change, those seeking the amendment will need not only prodigious skill but also a great deal of Luck. I wish them well. We wish, however, that the most reliable progress in improving the lot of the Aborigines will occur not at the pinnacle of Australian Legal System but through the decisions and actions of ordinary people in their everyday lives. If we view the Aboriginal society as Forest, we see most of the great trees felled by the troubled history of BLACK AND WHITE RELATIONS. CAN THAT ANCIENT FOREST THEN BE RECREATED? Can it be brought back to good health? Not in its original form- any more than an fallen tree be put back on its original stump.

In this state, there are some reasons to hope that the reasons of past failures are being learned. Unfortunately, many government projects did not succeed and everybody is bitter about the past failures.

From my knowledge, the story of the Aborigines is fraught with danger and must be handled carefully. We all hope the Aborigines people and the rest of Australia will be close and the these original people will one Day assume some power and, make their communities comfortable.

PART - 23

THE END OF POWER

I always assumed that power like Nature abhors a vacuum. In the history of World politics, there is always a talk of someone is bidding for hegemony. Today it is the United States, a century ago, it was Great Britain. Before that, it was French, the Spaniards. Before all these European nations, there were great civilizations of Asia and the Middle East.

The 19th century German historian Leopold Von Ranke, who started the study of Statecraft portrayed the modern European history as a constant struggle for mastery in which a balance of power was possible only through constant conflicts. Was this necessary or was it preconceived by some superpower? I have also come to believe most of the major occurrences in this world were primarily due to some conniving devil's plot. In history, it is always difficult to prove the guilt or innocence of some dictator.

It has become commonplace to observe that power is shifting all over the world. Today, it is the U.S. and we also acknowledge that wealth is now more concentrated than ever in the hands of very few rich people. Can the country control these people? I doubt it simply because there is too much freedom of movement and the money can be transferred easily and well hidden. I do not need to go in any details but the country's laws and the customs are to hide the personal wealth very easily.

Power, in other words, is not a National monopoly; the struggle for mastery is both perennial and universal. The "Unipolarity" identified by well - known commentators following the Soviet Union's collapse cannot last much longer, for the simple reason that history always hated Hyper-power. Sooner or later, challengers will arise and back we go to a Multi-polar World. In today's world, we have the dominance of the United States followed closely by China. But we are still Multi-polar.

But what if this view is wrong? What if the World is heading for a period when there is no hegemony? What if, instead of Balance of Power, there is an Absence of Power? Unfortunately, this situation is not totally unknown. A good case is the expiration of the Turkish Empire which left the entire area from Turkey to Egypt almost empty and without any rule at all. It left to the British and French Imperial powers to occupy this vast land and they divided into various countries including Israel. The entire division was done for making France and England rich and the entire history has been disastrous ever since.

Why might a power vacuum arise in the 21st century? From my present reading of the World affairs, it is not very hard to define. As usual, there are only few superpowers and the rest are trying desperately to catch them.

THE CLAY FEET OF THE COLOSSUS

(A) In my opinion, the U.S. suffers from few structural defects that will limit the effectiveness and duration of its World –power role in this world. The first is our dependence on foreign capital to finance private and public consumption. It is difficult to understand how the country can tolerate foreign aid for such a long time.

Secondly, the country is afflicted by attention deficit, its republic institutions have made it difficult to establish a consensus for long –term building projects. No congress wants to handle these projects as if nobody wants any long term projects.

(B) "Old Europe is getting older".

Some people dream the European Union could act as a counterweight to the U.S. should U.S. starts slumbering in International influence. With fertility rate dropping considerably all over Europe and life expectations are rising. the median weight of a normal European society will reach mid-forties. "old Europe" will really be old. A similar rough picture is painted for Japan where there is a growing shortage of manpower starting in the next 5 years.

(C) China's economic power - I am of the opinion that too much is made of China's economic might and China's GDP (Growth domestic power) will out -pace that of U.S. in the next few years.

(D) The Fragmentation of Islamic Civilization

With birthrates exploding all over the Middle East, there is bound to be a lot of pressure on Europe and U.S. to accommodate these people. There is lot of friction between Turkey and Arab countries, Between Shias and Sunnis Muslims, and Islamophobia, it is not easy to handle this complex problem.

In short, each of the obvious 21st century hegemons - the U.S., Europe, China seem to contain within the seeds of decline while Islam remains diffused, lacking a Superpower. The answer to this question is very difficult and our present wars all over the Middle East do not seem to go to any peaceful means.

I strongly feel we should not leave a lot of gap between U.S and anybody in the World. We should assume Global leadership because I fear the lack of leadership is dangerous to World's peace. After the first World War, the U.S. walked away in 1920 from assuming the leadership role under President Woodrow Wilson's power vacuum which caused the Bolshevik revolution in Russia and the beginning of the preparation of the Second World War.

The earlier history lesson goes back much many hundreds of years ago to show what happened when there was a gap in the world powers. In fact, in the 10th century – when the heirs of the Roman Empire- Rome and Byzantium had receded from the height of their power, when the Abbasid Caliphate was also waning, when the Chinese empire was languishing between the Tang and Sung dynasties in the absence of strong policies –it was the Religious Institutions –The Papacy in Rome, the Monastic orders, the Muslim Ulemas-that often set the Political agenda. That explains why the entire period culminated with the Holy War as the Crusades. Yet this clash of Civilizations was in many ways one more example of a Polar World susceptible to long distance military raids directed at the urban centers by less literate and backwards people. **Could this happen today**?

As I understand, the World is approaching a fork in the road. The inequality guaranteed by the love-growth climate has three primary elements: **Inequality of Wealth, Income and Opportunity.** The last of the three is manifested by **the Unemployment Numbers in** many European countries is the most EXPLOSIVE ELEMENT.

To add, it is also possible when you think for the inequality of opportunity, we tend to add, the fuel for political rage. This happened in the recent U.S. election when the majority of the ill - educated, poor lower class whites decided to vote for Trump and brought this nasty problem to its head once more. It is unfortunate that this country was not prepared for this absurd situation and even today, in May 2017 the country is still reeling from disaster.

Could a Polar World today produce an era of reminiscent of our troubled time? Certainly, one can imagine that the World's established powers retreating into their own regional spheres of influence. But what of the growing pretensions to autonomy under the supervision created by U.S. in 1940's such as IMF, World Bank, WTO etc. I suppose these Institutions represent the International Communities. Surely, their aspiration to global governance are, I hope, fundamentally different from the DARK AGES?

Today, this country is reeling from the ages of last thirty years where the gap between the rich and not rich has widened considerably. We had educational system where people are not educated and cannot find jobs in specialized fields. These angry people are the source of tomorrow's economic stability. Their main slogan widely publicized is "We will create trouble if we do not have decent jobs".

Have Universal claims become an integral part of our culture? All empires claim to rule the World, some totally unaware of the other civilizations in the World. The reality is political fragmentation. This is very much TRUE today! The defining characteristic of our age is not a shift of power upward to supranational institutions but DOWNWARD. It free flows of information and factors of production have empowered multi-national companies to say nothing of evangelistic cults of domination.

For the past two decades, globalization has been raising standards all over the world except where countries have shut themselves because of stupid civil wars. I feel, deglobalization would lead to Depression. The worst effects of the Dark ages would be felt on the margins of great powers such as U.S. and China. The prospect of a Polar world would frighten us. If U.S. would retreat from the role of global hegemony, its fragile self-belief dented by minor reversals – its critics would not pretend that they are ushering a new era of multi-polar harmony. The alternative to Unpolarity may not be Multi-polarity at all. **BECAREFUL WHAT YOU WISH FOR!**

PART - 24

DOING HISTORY ON A SWEEPING SCALE

Writing about history for the last 15 years has allowed me to make choices about the scale of history with which we are concerned. Historians differ fundamentally around the decisions they make about the scale. There are literally numerous examples of the discrepancy used by well-known historians in the last few years.

In my opinion, the concept of history plays a fundamental role is Human Thought. It invokes notions of human agency, change, the role of material circumstances in human affairs. It also raises the possibility of "**Learning from History**". This strongly suggests the possibility of better understanding ourselves in the present, by understanding the forces, choices and various circumstances that brought us to our current situations. It is, therefore, unsurprising that philosophers have selectively turned their attention to the efforts to examine History itself and the Nature of historical knowledge. I believe, these reflections can be grouped together into a body of work called **"PHILOSOPHY OF HISTORY".** Today, I presently enjoy reading such a heterogeneous group of analysts, idealists, logicians, academicians and others to read from an entirely different angle. This has become my current pursuit and hope to enjoy.

U.S. and Europe

Unlike most of the European critics of the U.S., I believe the World needs a liberal empire and U.S. is the best country for the job. The U.S. has good reasons to play the role of liberal Empire, both from the point of view of its own security and out of straight forward altruism. In many ways, the country is uniquely qualified to play this role, yet for all its colossal economic, military and cultural power, this country still looks to be an effective liberal empire without some profound structure in its economic structure, its social make-up and its domestic political culture. There are as usual many mysteries associated with every country but we have to decide to follow a country like U.S.

WHAT DOES AMERICA HAVE TO PAY ?

This is soon after the expiration since 1940 and it can do policing an unruly world than their British predecessors, the British Empire. On the whole, it was a very successful economic and political enterprise, well worth imitating. However, the U.S. is not suited nor does this country from flexing its muscles and making the world a better place. This country has three fundamental defects which makes it difficult to maintain its leadership:

(1) It is Economic Deficient.

(2) A Manpower deficit

(3) A HUGE ATTENTION deficit.

In my opinion, the Economic deficiency is remediable and may include risks down the road the country can withstand.

The Manpower deficit is problematic because Americans do not want to spend long years abroad serving their country. This is very unlike the British and the French who had their civil and military forces overseas for a very long time. This country cannot afford to have its forces or civil servants spend their lifetimes overseas. The American have very little tolerance and a high ATTAENTION DEFICIT.

THE GLOBAL EMPIRE

But an attention deficit may well be our undoing. We are the people sunk in unseemly denial. An American general's quote: We preach about values, democracy, human rights but we have not convinced ourselves that America cannot to preach a more asserting global role and not affect us".

We can try to understand that without the spread of British rule round the World, it is hard to believe that the structure of liberal capitalism would have been so successful in many different countries of the world. These countries which adopted an alternative like model like Chinese or Russian –imposed incalculable miseries on their people. It is also likely the Institute of Parliamentary Democracy could have been adopted by the majority of these countries.

In spite of all the selective economic stability and calm created by the British Empire, it so happens that this was also the Worst Empire in the World. They created two major world wars last century. This resulted in violent coming apart of multi-ethnic societies and the boom and bust Economic volatility. The British created the wars simply because they were afraid of German rise to power and superiority in technology and other ambitious programs.

Where does this take us. The World needs a stable political future where some disciplined countries have a solid economic background where the rest of the poor countries can depend on big and rich countries to help them financially. In this writer's opinion, that is the only way to maintain peace. This country with all its faults still has a big positive bearing on the rest of the World and a good U.S. president can really bring peace in today's world.

As mentioned earlier, my second look at my "New Philosophy of History" has opened a new vision and I am trying to use it to look at history in a different light and perspective.

PART - 25

RUSSIA —THE BEGINNING OF THE END OF THE SUPERPOWERSTATUS?

SECTION - 1

Moscow is still a superpower but its destructive politics is unsettling the international scenes and its behavior in the past few years makes one wonder whether it betrays its claim of a powerful nation. How should the West deal with Putin?

From the mid-19th century until the mid-20th century, the "German Question" was whether or not, a Unification of German under one rule would enter a powerful state at the center of Europe. This was decided in the end as Otto Von Bismarck had predicted by blood and iron. Two world wars brought violence and destruction in Europe and left Germany defeated and divided when it reunited in 1990, demographic decline and a cultural change had made few changes in Germany sufficiently strong enough the threat of a United Germany had receded.

The same cannot be said of Russia which has become more aggressive even as its economic significance has declined substantially in the past thirty years. The biggest question facing Europe today: What do we do about Russia?

Like the German question, the new Russian question is a function of the country's MITTELAGE its CENTRAL SITUATION. Germany's location was central in Europe. At its height, the German Reich extended from Koblenz to Koenigsberg, from the bank of Rhine in the North to the beaches of the Baltic.

Russia today is central in global terms. It was the only European Empire that extended from Asia to the North to Siberia in Europe. The old Soviet Union as we knew died about 25 years ago. Yet, today the Russian Federation still extends from Koeningberg to Vladivostock near Japan, about 4500 miles away and has 10 times zones. Russia's East p-West dilemma today is fast becoming he Central problem of International politics. On one side, lies China that long ago surpassed Russia in economic and demographic terms and has increased significantly in military power. On the side of Russia is Europe for all its prosperity has become political introverted and excessively reliant on United States for its dependence. This is big dilemma for Russia.

As I visualize today's World, there are four incompressible Conceptions in the world today: AMERICA, EUROPE, CHINA and ISLAMIC countries. RUSSIA'S PLACE IS VERY AMBIGUOUS. From "Peter the GREAT to Putin, circumstances have changed but the rhythm has remained consistent. Russia is uniquely European power sprawling across the two continents but never entirely out at home either in Asia or in Europe. It has learned its geo-politics from the Nord school of the Steppe where an army of nomadic lords contended for resources as an open terrain with few fixed borders.

I think, it is very easy to understand why Russia is least interested in World order. Historically, Russia always created trouble under the Communist rule. Last century, the Russians thought the communist philosophy would convert poor people in Asia and Europe to their way but this did not happen and Russia has been struggling for the past seventy years to regain some ground and it has failed miserably.

I personally think, Putin is least interested in peace either in Europe or other parts of the World. He is unable to Export his so-called, outdated communism anywhere in the world and the Russian economy is sinking rapidly. Russia put far too much emphasis on oil that they misguided its own advantage and with U. S. now being independent of foreign oil has dropped the oil prices considerably. But Putin is too stubborn to change it and Russia is like a third world country. As I remember the Russian economy has been in deficit for the past hundred years. Russia never developed the business strategy that really worked for the country. In its planning programs, there is not enough leverage to seize the advantage and continue on its way. But they do not work that way. If something does not work out, they still continue along the wrong way until the whole plan fails miserably. It happened with Nehru's first five years plan in India and unfortunately, they worked along the Russians planning and did not work too well.

The only way Putin can move is to damage Europe. He is coming out with stupid tricks to play cyberattacks during voting procedures. He played these stupid tricks in U.S. and French elections. Is this really the action of a Superpower or a third rate country. It seems Putin has a broad agenda to hurt the World wherever possible. He describes NATO as obsolete.

A NEW ERA BUT WHAT ERA?

It did not have to be this way. About 25 years ago, the dismantling of the old Soviet Union marked not only end of the cold war but also the beginning of what should have been golden age for the Soviet Russia and the West. It seems in the beginning Russia embraced both Capitalism and Democracy. It was starting to see Russian cities Westernized like St. Petersburg. A friend of mine told me he saw big differences from 1997 to 2000. The entire world be markedly more peaceful place as the flow of money and arms that had turned so many regional disputes were dried up. A number of American companies rushed to Russia to invest.

Now we go back to 1991 and imagine three or more likely features. It could not imagine the coup de by hard liners in August of that year by Putin and his gang that overthrew Gorbachev. This was well executed and overnight Russia was back its old way. Secondly, imagine a much more violent dissolution of the Soviet system in which ethnic and regional tensions escalated further, produced a kind of super-Yugoslavia which people did not want. Thirdly, imagine a happy era in which Russia's economy had flourished as the basis of Capitalism thus rivaling China.

Russia could have deep-frozen or could have been disintegrated. No one in 1991 knew which of these features Russia would adopt. In fact, we did not get any of them. Russia decided to retain national domestic institutes which were set up after 1991. But the rules of law did not roots and Putin established himself and suppressed opposition and criticism, Despite the Caucasus, the Russian federation was held together, and economy did not perform well than hoped. Between 1992 and 2016, the growth rate was 1,5%, Even India rate was 5.1 /5 and China was 8.9%.

Today the Russian economy accounts for just over 3 % of the Global Output according to IMF, China has 18 % and U.S about 17 %. Unfortunately, about 2/3 of Russian economy is based on Petroleum where the prices are falling every day. There is very little financial strength behind to revive the economy.

The world knows about Russia's severe problems but Russia makes all kinds of noises to divert the attention.

More will be discussed in SECTION 2.